DISCERNMENT

DISCERNMENT

A Study in Ecstasy and Evil

by
Morton Kelsey

PAULIST PRESS
New York/Ramsey/Toronto

Library of Congress
Catalog Card Number: 78-58958

ISBN 0-8091-2157-3

Published by Paulist Press
Editorial Office: 1865 Broadway, New York, N.Y. 10023
Business Office: 545 Island Road, Ramsey N.J. 07446

Printed and bound in the
United States of America

Contents

*To my friend
and able discerner of spirits,
Jack Sanford*

Preface

How can one discern the touch of God upon one's life? For many years I have pondered that question. I went through college and seminary without receiving help in solving the problem. Then in a period of conflict and confusion I discovered the reality of my own inner world. It practically forced itself upon me. I also discovered that some very mature and knowledgeable people believed that we were surrounded by and contained in a spiritual world as well as a physical one. If this were true then the problem of discerning how God touched my life became much simpler.

At this same time I also learned that the forces of evil were very real indeed. But I learned an even more important truth. There was another aspect of spiritual reality which could and did rescue me from that evil. It was very often in my confrontations with inner evil that I came to realize most powerfully the reality and availability of Love, God, a Rescuer.

As I began to speak in my parish of the reality of the spiritual world and of the New Testament as a guidebook for dealing with it, the parish began to come to life. Soon I found I was asked to lecture on this subject. I wrote several articles describing these experiences. One of them was published some time later by Dove Publications of the Benedictine Monastery at Pecos, New Mexico, and was entitled *The Reality of the Spiritual World*. A second article I prepared for a conference at Lake Arrowhead arranged by the Extension Division of the University of California at Los Angeles. On that weekend Alan Watts and I took opposing views on the subject of evil. My remarks were published in the January 1974 issue of *The Journal of Religion and Health*. A third article was originally delivered under the title *Intervening with Meaning* at the symposium on "The Role of the Christian Churches in the Recovery of the Alcoholic," in Milwaukee in April of 1974. It was later published as a pamphlet by

1

Dove Publications with the title *Finding Meaning: Guidelines for Counselors.*

It was my friend and editor at Paulist Press, Richard Payne, who suggested that these various studies had a common thread. In each of them I was looking at the subject of discernment. With this in mind I went back through these papers and found that he was correct. I began to realize the importance of this subject in the renewal which is sweeping many parts of the church. With a great deal of additional writing and extensive editing the present book took shape.

I am deeply grateful to my wife Barbara who encouraged me to complete this work during a summer vacation and also for her careful reading and editing of my typescript.

I am grateful to Paisley Roach who worked with me on the original articles and who has helped put the book in final form. Max Zeller, Hilde Kirsch and James Kirsch were real friends and guides as I hammered out a world-view in which my Christianity was relevant to the modern world. They were for me prophetic figures who opened my eyes to the reality of the spiritual world and the significance of the New Testament in dealing with it. Leo Froke and I discussed most of the ideas presented here over a long period of time. He has a real gift of discernment. Most of the ideas have also been discussed with my friend Andy Canale. The friendship of Jack Sanford has been one of the great gifts to me over the last twenty years. His clarity of discernment has helped me with the ideas we have discussed and even more important he has listened to me and offered me discernment about who I am and where I should be going. I am grateful to Peter Dean for the picture of the soul on page 122.

I am grateful to Carmela Rulli and her stenographic staff at the University of Notre Dame for putting this manuscript in usable form.

August 1977
Gualala, California

Chapter I
What Is Discernment?

We live in an age of spiritual fads. There is a reaction to the materialism of the nineteenth century and the first part of the twentieth century. The young are fed up with the gray flannel suit culture of Madison Avenue. Older people are retiring earlier. Men and women are seeking for something, looking for the pot of gold at the end of the rainbow. There is a rising hope that there may be a treasure there after all. There may be meaning, ecstasy, union with the cosmos or even love which is more powerful than evil and destructiveness.

The Gallup Poll recently did a survey on the forms of religious practice that Americans of the nineteen seventies are using. They found that at least four percent (4%) of the populace have tried Transcendental Meditation, three percent (3%) have used one form of yoga or another and two percent (2%) have been touched by the Charismatic Renewal. Andrew Greeley did a survey in 1974 and discovered that thirty-nine percent (39%) of a random sample of Americans believed that they had had mystical experiences which took them out of themselves and brought them into relationship with a spiritual reality greater than they. Most of them had never told anyone about these experiences because of cultural disbelief. The last person they would be likely to tell about such things, Greeley found, would be professional religious people because these people, they felt, don't believe in such things anymore.[1]

A similar survey run by *Psychology Today* brought answers from 40,000 readers. Nearly sixty percent (60%) maintained that they had had such experiences according to the November 1974 issue of that magazine. Again few of these people find help among the "standard-brand" churches or their ministers.

Adam Smith's best seller, *Powers of Mind*, gives a picture

3

of the spiritual techniques that modern Westerners are using. His accurate, knowledgeable and witty presentation reveals the hunger for something more of those brought up in a behavioristic culture. And then there is the amazingly wide use of hallucinogenic drugs, marijuana and stronger, among the young and not so young. As Andrew Weil has pointed out so clearly in *The Natural Mind*, the basic motivation of most drug users is in a real sense religious. They are trying to escape from ordinary space-time existence into something larger and find little help in official religion and so go their own way with drugs. At the same time there is a growing interest in ESP and the powers of the mind which give contact with more than physical realities. There is an interest in possible communication with the deceased supported by responsible writers like Dr. Raymond Moody and Dr. Elisabeth Kübler-Ross. The Greeley survey indicated that twenty-five percent (25%) of their sample believed that they had had some contact with the deceased.

In the Charismatic Renewal there are reports of the action of God in the lives of people today. Tongue speaking was the hallmark of the early renewal. Since then there have been prophecies, healings, gifts of wisdom and knowledge, visions and many other physical effects attributed to the divine. One of the most interesting of these is the phenomenon of "slaying in the spirit." This is found in many charismatic groups in which individuals collapse when touched by the leader and lie prostrate upon the ground. There is renewed interest in exorcism, the expelling of destructive spiritual entities from human beings.

Amid this welter of experiences the average individual is quite understandably confused. Few churches have clergy well enough trained in such matters to be of much help to people. What is not understood in religious circles is often dismissed as non-existent or as coming from the devil. I have shown in my book, *The Christian and the Supernatural*, that most clergy and churches react in one of these two ways. What is needed is some discernment or clear recognition of the value and source of these experiences. Where do they come from? Are they illusions that are only disguised physical experiences? Do they arise from the depth of the human psyche? Are they therefore merely human experiences? Do these phenomena arise from contact with a neutral spiritual environment that extends beyond the borders of the human psyche? Or do they come from some malignant spiritual reality bent upon destroying us human beings? Or are they actually signs of God's action in our lives?

The Need for Discernment

The early church knew the need for discernment. The early Christians lived in a world which was surprisingly like our own. There was a pervasive belief in spiritual entities or beings, both good ones and evil ones, which influenced human lives. Paul saw the ability to discern or recognize the value and source of spiritual experiences as a gift itself. In the paraphrase of the New Testament entitled *Good News for Modern Man*, the gift of discerning spirits is translated as "the ability to tell the difference between gifts that come from the Spirit and those which do not." This certainly gives the essential meaning which Paul was trying to convey. Paul was not particularly interested in pinning down the source of a supposed more-than-human ability; he was concerned, however, with being able to recognize clearly (the exact dictionary meaning of discern) which experiences were the result of the Spirit of God, the Holy Spirit, the third person of the Trinity. He didn't want attributed to the Spirit what was either human or demonic in nature.

Paul has several lists of gifts scattered throughout his letters. In 1 Corinthians 12 he describes nine gifts. These gifts are special graces or gifts (*charismáta* in Greek) given by the Spirit to enable Christians to get about the task of living and spreading the Gospel. In this passage he speaks of the gifts of wisdom and knowledge, the gifts of healing and miracles, of faith, of prophecy, tongues and interpretation of tongues, and then the gift of discernment. In Romans 12:6 Paul writes of some gifts which seem to be less glamorous than the others: the gifts of preaching, service, teaching, encouragement, sharing, authority (administration) and showing kindness. In Ephesians 4:11 there is still another list which speaks of those who are "gifted" to be apostles, prophets, evangelists, pastors and teachers.

It was extremely important in the early church to discern

which apostles and prophets spoke through the Spirit and which ones spoke from their own human motivation or through a "lying" or deceitful spirit. The church was set upon and attacked from every side, by the civil authority as well as by enthusiasts within the fellowship who wished to take it over. If the church were to survive it had to know which of the movements within its life came from the Spirit and which were coming from some other quarter.

Gifts are indeed given. They are special graces given for the upbuilding of the church. But the gift can either be used, developed and enhanced or it can be left fallow. In most human gifts there is a human element. Again it was a very important matter to know when the prophet spoke from God and whether the healings and miracles came from his Spirit. For nearly three centuries the church struggled against persecution. One of the reasons it survived was that it was given special help, special grace, and it treasured and used that help.

We find ourselves in a world in many ways similar to that ancient world. Old patterns of living had broken down and people were looking for experiences which carried some meaning and life for them. The church found it necessary to develop the gift of discernment to guide its members through the many spiritual experiences offered by that world. One of the main tasks of pastors and prophets, evangelists and administrators was to discern which things came from the Spirit and which things came from other sources, and then to guide those coming into the fellowship of the church upon a path which led to a living fellowship with the Risen Christ.

In our own day, however, the church has been so overwhelmed with rationalism and materialism that it has not seen any particular need for discernment. When religion is a matter of morality and rational and inferred faith, one does not need discernment. If humankind is simply caught in a physical space-time existence, then all experiences of something beyond that world, good or bad, are to be discounted. If human beings have mind-psyches which are quite simple and easily understood and contribute little to experience other than recording it, then again discernment is simply not relevant to the work of the modern church. It is really quite silly to train ministers to function in what are considered non-existent areas, and therefore seminaries provide little or no training in such understanding. Thus the church has little to say about the new interests in spiritual reality and the ways of perceiving it which have become so much a part of the current religious scene.

Eastern religions have attracted great numbers of people seeking spiritual experiences. One reason, which has been described by Harvey Cox in his book *Turning East*,[2] is that the religions of the East have maintained a belief in the spiritual world and have kept alive practices for relating to that world. They may have ignored the physical world as illusion, but they are themselves certain of spiritual realities. They have methods of discerning good practices from dangerous ones and offer disciplines to lead one on the somewhat perilous inner journey. *The Tibetan Book of the Dead* suggests that one needs all the discernment one can get as one steps out of life into the *bardo*, which is the realm of existence between incarnations.

Understanding Discernment

There is a clear need in twentieth-century Christian circles for learning to use the gift of discernment and for admitting candidates for ministry who have this gift. Christian ministers (using that term in the broadest possible meaning) need to learn how to discern. Often I am called in South Bend by ministers, both Catholic and Protestant, with parishioners who are having mystical and paranormal experiences. Rationalistic theology offers no criteria for dealing with these phenomena and they do not know what to do with either the parishioners or the experiences. No wonder Andrew Greeley reports that those with mystical experiences would turn last of all to the standard-brand religious professionals. Raymond Moody reports the same kind of experience from those who have had "death experiences" and have returned to tell about them.

In order to explain some of the ABC's of discernment we shall begin by taking a close look at the phenomenon of slaying in the spirit. This experience is relatively recent as a widespread experience among charismatic Christians. It is a practical and concrete example of the need for discernment. We shall first look at the experience as it is described and as I have seen it. We shall try to place this experience within the context of religious history and then provide a theological and psychological framework for this experience. We shall add some guidelines for dealing with this phenomenon. This will show the necessity for developing some theoretical ideas about discernment.

We shall then go on to a broader discussion of the whole subject of the angelic and the demonic. There is little sensibly written on this subject, and so we must start practically from scratch to describe the nature of the spiritual world and the nature of ontological evil (evil that has real substance and reality), the Evil One in particular. This will require a good bit of historical and theological material. However, if there are gifts and if they can be given by the demonic as well as the angelic, by the spirit of destruction as well as by the Spirit, it is terribly important to know about it. It is equally important not to attribute to his infernal majesty gifts and abilities that are natural or merely neutral abilities. This would result in a constricted view of human beings and human nature.

We shall then sketch out a tentative model for Christian psychology. In order to discern what comes of the Spirit one must know something of the nature and structure of the human being. Men and women are far more complex than we ordinarily think. They have more capacities to know than we ordinarily believe. In order to practice wise discernment it is necessary to have some picture of the development, depth, complexity and potential of the human psyche. If the human being contributes something to experience other than recording objectively what is out beyond one, then discernment requires that we ascertain what human beings contribute to experience. We shall then show the kind of discernment necessary to lead lost human beings to meaning and hope.

In conclusion let us summarize the reasons for venturing to discuss the subject at hand. Discernment is necessary because there is a real spiritual world with elements that are neutral, elements that are destructive, and elements that protect one and lead one to God. Discernment is necessary because we are very complicated human beings. We have a physical body of incredible complexity and a psychic aspect to our humanness that is even more intricate. In order to be sure that gifts come from God we must be quite certain that they do not arise in the depth and complexity of our humanness. Discernment requires clear thinking and as wide a knowledge of the history of religion as is possible. There are few things new under the sun and historical knowledge can often guide our discernment and keep us from error and folly. Let us turn to the Charismatic Renewal and the phenomenon of "slaying in the spirit" which has arisen within it.

Chapter II
Slaying in the Spirit:
The Place of Trance and Ecstasy
in Christian Experience

In these changing times the deepest and most dramatic change of all is taking place within human beings. A new attitude toward human experience can be observed in fields as diverse as modern physics, sociology, psychiatry, and anthropology. In 1969 the study of parapsychology was accepted as a full-fledged science by the American Association for the Advancement of Science. More and more students are writing about extrasensory perception, meditation, demonism, abilities to heal and to see into the future, and related subjects.

The same change of attitude has spread within the church. The Pentecostal revival which began early in this century has come to influence all the major Protestant churches and is now having a dramatic impact within the Catholic Church. Twenty-five years ago how many of us would have believed that the Christian churches we seemed to know so well would soon be attracting national attention by the religious phenomena they produced? Few people would have even guessed that religious books would make a comeback after the tremendous decline of interest in the postwar period. Instead religious publishing has surged ahead until it now ranks as big business.

Although many of the traditional churches have tended to ignore or disparage the Pentecostal or Charismatic Renewal, others have seen a renewal of the church itself in this new emphasis on personal experience of religion. No group has worked harder to integrate this new experience than the Catholic Church under the careful guidance of Cardinal Suenens. One of the best studies of these experiences, of how they can be understood theologically and approached by pastors, is found in the Malines' document produced by a group of scholars and published in Belgium.[1] Cardinal Suenens has carried out the implications of this paper. In his book *A New Pentecost?* he shows how Vatican II opened the door to a new vision of experiential Christianity, and how the charismatic movement has picked up this vision and given it life and expression.

This new attitude toward religious experience has been encouraged by people who have found renewal and meaning through experiences within a religious framework. Almost overnight a great many individuals have discovered new reasons for taking part in the church. In the past hardly anyone expected direct, observable results from the traditional practices of organized religion. But along with the charismatic experience has come a belief in the possibility of direct contact with God, based on the experience of *charismata* or gifts which we mentioned earlier. This movement has produced sober, often carefully detailed reports of healings, prophecies, visions, and miracles, as well as speaking in tongues, interpretation of tongues, and also a seemingly new phenomenon known as "slaying in the spirit." There are also reports of transforming effects upon the lives of some of those who have these experiences.

Most of these phenomena have been explored in some depth by many writers. I have dealt with four of them in four of my books.[2] The most dramatic of them, however, has not received the same attention. Until recently slaying in the spirit was seen almost entirely in emotionally packed evangelic situations, in camp meetings and revivals. Then with the ministry of Kathryn Kuhlman this experience became known to many more people, and before long it was occurring in other religious circles, both Protestant and Catholic. Many neo-Pentecostal groups have accepted slaying in the spirit as the mark of an individual's openness to religious experience. There are even those in various groups who state that they have a special ministry in providing this experience to people.

Slaying in the spirit is an unusual and powerful phenomenon which demands careful and thorough consideration. None of these gifts and experiences can be approached offhand if we are to understand their proper place in people's lives and how they can be used as true *charismata*. God's purposes in giving his gifts are not always easy for us human beings to learn or to put into effect. In addition there are other psychic experiences that can come to the most devout and orthodox Christians and require much the same understanding. The church is naturally cautious about such things as hearing voices or sensing touches, odors or tastes that seem to come from outside agents.[3] By trying to understand the experiences that are generally accepted as charismatic, we can help to build an approach to many of these phenomena and develop a way of discerning what in these experiences comes from the Spirit.

We shall therefore examine slaying in the spirit in some depth. Since there is apparently more to this startling experience than meets the eye, we shall consider a number of descriptions of what it looks like from the outside, and then from the inside and from the minister's point of view. Next we shall try to see where there have been similar occurrences in religious history, particularly in biblical times. We shall follow these phenomena through the later history of our religion where slaying in the spirit, spoken of in various ways, is found again and again among 'enthusiastic" religious groups. These experiences were well known and well documented especially in the early days of Methodism in England and in the massive revivals of the eighteenth and nineteenth centuries in the United States. By our own century they were expected among groups known as "Holy Rollers," usually among the uneducated and socially deprived who also told of healings and other gifts of the spirit. These experiences originally gave the "Quakers" and the "Shakers" their very names.

With this background we shall then look at the psychology of religious trances and conversion experiences. The purposes of this study must be clearly understood at the outset. Our effort will be to understand the nature and depth of the human psyche and our capacity for receiving and benefiting from experiences like these, not in any way to deny or debase the meaning and value of the experiences themselves. By learning about ourselves we can also discover a great deal about the meaning of the experiences and thus about their source. In addition we can learn to distinguish between creative and possibly dangerous expressions of the experiences. Fr. George Maloney has shown the need for such discernment with great clarity; he writes in a recent article on slaying in the spirit:

> As in all such phenomena that involve a delicate interaction of body-soul-spirit, one can hardly attribute such "slaying in the Spirit" totally to God's Holy Spirit without due discernment, nor totally to one's own psychic powers, nor totally to demonic control. Discernment is always needed.
> And the more a psychic phenomenon has dramatic repercussions upon one's body, all the greater care must be taken.[4]

We shall continue with an evaluation of the experience of 'slaying" based on the insights gained from considering these historical, religious and psychological materials. In conclusion we shall consider some specific suggestions for dealing with the experience so that it may result in growth and development for both the individual and the church, rather than causing problems, division and misunderstanding. These suggestions, which are made to help pastors and lay people find an approach to slaying in the spirit, will apply to various other psychic phenomena as well.

The Experience

My first experience of something similar to slaying occurred about ten years ago at a healing conference which Agnes Sanford and I conducted in the midwest. As is customary at the end of these conferences, we were holding a dedication service in which each participant received the laying-on-of-hands. As I laid my hands upon a minister who was kneeling before me, he slumped to the floor and seemed to lose consciousness. We ministered to him and in a few minutes he "came to" and we continued the service. Although none of us had expected this to happen, I was not particularly concerned or upset. I knew that the individual was in good health, and in the research for my book on tongue speaking I had read of experiences like this in the history of Methodism. I also realized how fragile our attainment of consciousness is and how easily it can vanish into thin air when our emotions are particularly vivid and running high.

From all that I could learn from the minister at that time and later on, this was a valuable experience for him. He felt that it was a spiritual dying and rising which gave him a new start on the religious way. Later I was told of a similar experience by a friend in the ministry who was using laying-on-of-hands for healing and was surprised when one person apparently fainted dead away and then seemed to feel better than before. At the time I had not even heard of the ministry of Kathryn Kuhlman.

Several years after this, at the suggestion of Agnes Sanford, I went to the Shrine Auditorium in Los Angeles to attend one of Miss Kuhlman's healing services. This time I was expecting an encounter with slaying in the spirit. I went with an open mind, fairly well prepared by twenty years in an active, though less dramatic healing ministry. The parking area, I found, was packed; buses had brought people from as far as two hundred miles away. Inside there were over twelve thousand, waiting with obvious openness and expectancy. As the services began, the singing was contagious, and Kathryn Kuhlman's movements and speaking created almost an electric atmosphere. There were a number of healings reported from all over the great hall. Then people came forward to be slain in the spirit.

As Miss Kuhlman put out her hand and touched the forehead of the first person (who happened to be a man), he slumped backward and was caught by two attendants who placed him gently on the floor. Quietly Miss Kuhlman moved to the next person, and on down the long line, and nearly everyone she touched fell, apparently unconscious. No one was hurt. Each one was lowered to the floor, lay absolutely still for a few minutes, and then got up and walked calmly back to his or her seat. Now and then there was someone who did not have this unusual and quite dramatic experience, but one had to be watching to tell for sure which ones did or did not have the experience.

Again I was not greatly surprised. From all that I saw and what I knew about the history of revivalism and about the dynamics of the human personality, I felt that this particular ministry was reaching these people in a very real way. It appeared in essence to be a sincere and genuine effort to reach out to human need. The enthusiasm was well channeled and things were done decently and in order. Since then I have come across several people who received dramatic and permanent healings at services held by Kathryn Kuhlman. Although this extraverted way of bringing religious feelings into the open does not minister to my own particular type of personality, I have found it real and valuable for various people and I encouraged some of my congregation to attend her services if they felt an inclination to do so.

Let us listen to descriptions by several other individuals in order to get a more comprehensive view of these experiences. In his book *Psychic Healers* David St. Clair writes:

Then Kathryn Kuhlman did something extraordinary. She reached out and prayed for the woman, but as her fingers touched the woman's forehead, the woman fell backward. She seemed to be jolted by an unexpected lightning bolt that knocked her off her feet and into the waiting arms of one of Miss Kuhlman's helpers. She lay there, on the stage, for a few seconds before regaining consciousness. When they helped her to her feet, she, still in tears, thanked Miss Kuhlman again. "It is not me, my dear, that you must thank," said the evangelist. "I have no power. It is the power of Jesus that cured you. Please don't give me your praise. Give it to the Lord." And she reached out again, and again the woman fell over backward onto the floor.[5]

George Maloney writes about being on the stage at Kuhlman meetings, and then describes his own experience the first time he was an instrument of a slaying:

I have been on the stage when Miss Kuhlman had two healing services before 4,500 charismatic people assembled in Jerusalem from all parts of the world. People who came to the stage declared to her and to the audience that Jesus Christ had healed them, through Miss Kuhlman. She put her hands under each person's chin and nearly everyone fell backward into the hands of her aides . . .

I remember the first time someone fell while I was praying in a healing service. I wondered why the usher stood behind the row of persons who wanted to be prayed over and held a large, black blanket. The first, a little old lady, fell backward as I prayed over her. Solemnly the usher covered her body with the blanket and she lay there a full ten minutes with a beatific smile on her face before she stirred and sat down. Every Saturday someone was "slain" in the Spirit and people to some degree wanted it to happen. It seemed to happen readily to those who wanted it to happen and who easily could "let go" and merely let it happen.[6]

What, then, does this experience mean to the person who is having it? The following report comes from a woman who is Catholic and a member of the charismatic movement. She describes her own experience at a healing service conducted by a well-known Catholic healer:

When the time arrived for the "slaying in the Spirit" ceremony, we had learned a little bit about what to expect in his talk, and I honestly was open to the working of the Lord. At first it seemed unreal to see people going up, being touched and prayed over, then falling down, and a little later just casually getting up and returning to their seats. A few were more emotional than others. After a few minutes it all just seemed natural. When it was my turn I felt a little self-conscious, thinking of what I might do. But when he touched my shoulder and prayed I lost my self-consciousness and felt myself going down, although I was aware of going down. I didn't really worry about hitting the floor. However, after I was down a few seconds I promptly got up, so maybe my self-consciousness returned. However, it was a peaceful feeling and I returned to my seat filled with calm contentment and I felt as though I had been lifted a little out of space and wanted to stay there for a while. It was truly a religious experience and I would neither encourage it nor discourage it as I feel it should be done only in the appropriate circumstances with the proper person ministering such to the people.[7]

Several people have discussed the effects of this experience with me in an effort to understand what had happened to them. One very cultivated and discerning woman, for instance, had gone up for the laying-on-of-hands feeling open and wanting to find out what God could do through her. She described what took place as suddenly not caring whether she stayed on her feet or not, then abandoning herself to God knowing that she would be cared for. Perhaps, she suggested, there was a momentary lapse of awareness as she fell, like the haziness in a petit mal seizure. But she did not describe anything like real loss of consciousness. She was quite aware of lying on the floor feeling open and close to God, in very real communion with him. She concluded that what she had experienced was a loss of *self-*consciousness; apparently during those moments she had let go of conscious ego control and given over that responsibility to other hands.

Most people describe this phenomenon as giving in, submitting to God or the Holy Spirit. Sometimes they speak of being scared and cold, even feeling "goose bumps" as a hand touches them, while many others feel warmth flowing through them. Either way they generally describe a sense of holy power or energy flowing in, which makes them relax and fall, bringing peace and joy. As Fr. Maloney shows:

> A "floating" effect accompanies the falling to earth, filling the receiver with a sense of deep peace and joy. The whole body, soul and spirit seem to "let go" under an invisible power. This state of relaxation on all levels, with the body in a very loose condition, accounts for falls with rarely any physical mishaps accompanying them.[8]

One friend who is a scientist has given me quite a detailed report of his experiences with slaying in the spirit. Over the years I have learned to trust both his analytical ability and his Christian experience. This is his account:

> I have "gone down under the power" twice, both times in the same meeting. My wife and I were at a meeting led by Charles and Frances Hunter. . . . There was an altar call for

couples who wanted God to bless their marriage. Perhaps twenty-five or more couples went forward. We stood before the altar in a semi-circle. One of the Hunters stretched out his/her arm. Nearly simultaneously, all of us gently fell backward, caught by men who had come forward, and were lowered to the floor.

Later in the evening, Charles called for those who needed healing or wished to stand in for others. I had been asked to stand in for a young woman who could not attend. I was standing in her stead, felt myself falling backward, wondered if anyone was there to catch me, said "so what," and found myself lying comfortably on the floor. In both cases I was fully conscious at all times. I did not feel anything occurring internally, yet I did not care to rise for ten to fifteen minutes. Subsequent observation brought no marked changes; however, the young lady expressed a lessening of a burden corresponding to the time of my standing-in. She could not have known of that hour, being about 125 miles away. . . .

This man had known of Kathryn Kuhlman's ministry and had attended her services and seen the phenomenon in Pittsburgh. Later he became involved in almost weekly occurrences of slaying in the Pentecostal church he attended in Kansas. He continues:

An evangelist from Oklahoma was invited to conduct a "Revival" in the church. . . . Some three or four nights into his campaign, some people, upon being prayed for, went "down under the Power." As far as I could determine, this phenomenon was not previously known by the congregation although the evangelist and the pastor were familiar with it. There was no teaching accompanying the events although I was asked for biblical references. (John 18:6 is the closest reference I can locate.) Soon the meetings appeared to be pointing toward this phenomenon: the evangelist was asked to stay on an additional four weeks (beyond the original two).

My wife and I discontinued going. . . . The subsequent months have seen a continuation of these events. The common denominators appear to be: 1. The pastor calls for those requesting prayer and usually names specific needs. 2. Nearly always the same people come forward, teens, children and adults. 3. The pastor prays and lays a hand on the individual. 4. The same people have the same problems. . . .

Although there is often a remarkable similarity in describing what takes place, as one talks with those who have been slain in the spirit and observes them, it becomes apparent that this experience cannot be exhausted in any simple description. What the outside observer sees is one thing. It looks as if the individual is going into a swoon or faint, loses consciousness and then finally comes to. Unless some vision or other content is reported, there is usually no sign of anything different.

What the participant experiences, on the other hand, is not so much a loss of consciousness as a loss of control. The person loses control of the ability to stand. The psychological forces involved are very complex, as parents with small children will probably realize. One lets go and falls down, in nearly every instance with a sense of being cared for by God, either totally or at any rate as far as one's physical control is concerned. How this experience affects an individual will probably depend upon the psychological condition as well as the relationships, understanding and general situation of that person. Like any other human experience, there is really no simple description that will do justice to slaying in the spirit. The best one can do is to say that something passes from one human being to another which apparently brings the second individual into touch with another dimension of reality, causing that person to let go of ordinary conscious control and thus fall to the ground. If not actually unconscious of ordinary reality, the individual is at least focusing attention almost entirely upon this other level of reality.

Let us consider next how this experience appears to the person who is ministering it. We shall look first at a brief account by a Pentecostal minister and then at a careful analysis by a Catholic priest who worked with the phenomenon for some time.

*A Personal History of Ministering
Slaying in the Spirit*

In a tape entitled "Why Do People Fall Under the Power?"
the Rev. Kenneth Hagin, an evangelist and healer in Tulsa,
Oklahoma, describes his experience in a Pentecostal meeting:

> Like a powerful current passing through an electric wire, I
> felt the anointing of the Holy Spirit come upon me so pow-
> erfully that I ran down the aisle touching thirty-five people
> with my one finger on their forehead, and down fell all of
> them to the ground. Seventeen who had not received the
> baptism of the Holy Spirit spoke in tongues when they rose
> from the floor.

While one can learn something about this ministry from
descriptions like this, there is need for further understanding as
the following account shows. It is drawn from the experiences
and the reflections of a priest who is active in the Catholic
charismatic movement, and whom I have known for a number of
years. During the time that his ministry involved slaying in the
spirit we kept in close contact and had many discussions of the
experience. He has given me permission to use the paper he
wrote about this ministry and any material from our discussions.
  Like so many others, this priest first became acquainted
with slaying through the ministry of Kathryn Kuhlman. He
attended with David Geraets, Abbot of the Benedictine
Monastery in Pecos, New Mexico, and the two found themselves
on the front row of the stage. As he describes:

> I had been briefed before the service began and said a prayer
> to the Lord to help me to be open to everything, and when I
> heard about the Slaying in the Spirit I eagerly looked for-
> ward to experiencing it. After most of the service, as was
> usual, she turned to us clergy and began to go down the row
> touching them and as she did they fell. I couldn't wait! But,
> much to my chagrin when she came to David and myself
> nothing happened; but she did pray a special prayer of
> anointing over us. Following that I was very disappointed

and immediately began questioning David who said very succinctly, "It doesn't happen to some people." I still didn't give up because we were going to have the privilege of meeting Miss Kuhlman backstage through the courtesy of Mr. Tom Lewis. And, sure enough, beginning at the other end of the circle she proceeded to touch people and they all fell. Again, when she got to David and me nothing happened. I then decided that it wasn't supposed to happen to me and it never did. I attended several other Kathryn Kuhlman services and always tried to be open despite her flamboyant manner. I, too, like so many others, loved her statement, "There's so much more!" In that way she began to be an ideal of Christian ministry.

During the following summer he went to a priests' retreat where he met a woman almost as extraordinary as Kathryn Kuhlman herself. He had an opportunity to meet with this leader alone for prayer, and during that time he had the following, most powerful experience:

We went up to the sanctuary steps and knelt. She prayed over me and it seemed I experienced what St. Paul talks about as "leaving the body." At any rate, it was quite overwhelming and I never experienced such a sense of deep peace; I was oblivious to everyone and everything around me. I became conscious again when I heard her praying over my hands asking the Lord to anoint them afresh with his healing power. She then gave me a prophecy directing me to heal any who were to come to me. To say that it was a tremendous experience at the time is an understatement. But when I got home I was in for a real surprise.

At his first regular service with laying-on-of-hands for healing he found that his hands burned and his palms began to peel. And then people began to fall to the floor as he prayed over them. This came as a bolt out of the blue. He could not remember any suggestion that this would happen to him. He called me and also talked with a few friends in the charismatic movement, but he found no real guidelines for working with the experiences that people were having.

In spite of an inner urge to be cautious, he grew more and more excited about what was happening because it seemed to bear good fruit most of the time. Sometimes there were adverse reactions, but he considered that these people were simply closed to the Spirit. Often there were "prophecies," and many people seemed to find great release and joy. A day of renewal had been planned, and he decided that this experience was just what was needed. As a result about five hundred were slain in the spirit, and the effects seemed overwhelming. Some people admitted that they had come up to test the experience with no intention of being slain, and were overwhelmed nonetheless. Later, reflecting back, he realized that there had been a violent negative reaction on the part of one priest and that three women had become hysterical, but these were judged as "demonic manifestations." He also learned that several people had simply walked out, but decided that this indicated a lack of commitment to Christ which made these individuals uncomfortable in the presence of such a display of God's power.

People began to identify slaying in the spirit with this priest, and soon it was happening almost every time he prayed with people. Sometimes individuals would fall to the floor when he walked into a room where a prayer meeting was to be held. Attendance at the prayer meetings tripled. Enthusiasm kept mounting, building toward a climax about a year after the experiences began. Another day of renewal was to be held, and he brought in an outside leader to work with him. They talked over the fact that some of the clergy and laity were openly displeased at what was happening, and they decided to discourage any occurrence of the experience. During the meeting, however, the outside leader felt called, as if anointed, to ask people to come forward for prayer. Starting with my priest friend, the power of slaying in the spirit spread like wildfire through the whole group of priests who were officiating and praying for people. Hundreds of people came forward and had the experience. Needless to say, this made for a very enthusiastic crowd.

The next day the priest's bishop stepped in. Through the vicar for clergy, he was asked to discontinue this ministry. In effect it was a cease and desist order. Of course he followed it, but at a cost of considerable conflict and confusion. He wanted to prove the bishop wrong and wrote to several authorities for evidence. One of them was George Maloney, the Jesuit priest whose paper we have quoted. Fr. Maloney wrote back a strong letter urging caution, mentioning that he had studied under a Jewish parapsychologist who could do the same thing without any reference to God. My priest friend did not like this letter and chose to ignore its advice until later.

Gradually, however, he came to have less and less enthusiasm for this ministry. Finally he had a personal interview with the bishop who expressed the very sensible point of view that, because of the sensationalism surrounding it, slaying in the spirit ought to be avoided if for no other reason than to keep from hurting the Renewal movement. He spoke about adverse experiences he had had with the phenomenon in another diocese. On the other hand, he conceded, if it happened in private prayer with people without being promoted, it obviously could not be avoided.

A few months later the priest had an opportunity to meet with David du Plessis at a charismatic conference and ask him about this experience. To his surprise this Pentecostal leader who is known around the world minced no words. As this priest wrote,

[Du Plessis] told me unequivocally to stay clear of slaying in the spirit entirely—that in all of his years of Pentecost all over the world he had never seen it build up the Church but rather cause discredit to the classical Pentecostals. It was one reason for the derisive name "holy rollers." He also said that he had the same reservations about people who practiced it, especially if they made slaying in the spirit the focus of their whole ministry. In a fatherly way he beseeched me to leave it alone. He also added the very sobering admonition that he felt strongly that the Spirit was not calling Catholics to imitate classical Pentecostals—much less their mistakes—but to be authentic Catholics who are open to the Spirit. He said it was important for us to discover the Spirit *within* our own traditions!

This attitude, coming from a leader who is admired by so many people, reinforced the bishop's injunction and made this particular priest stop to reflect deeply upon his experience. He came up with some realizations. First of all, it became apparent to him that this experience depended to a large extent on the frame of mind or psychological state of the person ministering it to others. When one was "high" it happened easily, but let him become burdened or depressed and his ability to bring the experience to others was noticeably diminished. He began to see how much effect our own psyches can have on this ministry.

Then there was the feeling of exhaustion, which he had tried to ignore, that so often came after ministering in this way. Being exposed to these experiences seemed to drain energy and power from him. Sometimes, he realized, a sense of caution or even fear had overtaken him and he had tried to get away from the scene as soon as he could. It was also strange that the attendants, simply waiting to catch those who fell, could affect what happened. Sometimes one of them had touched either him or the next person in line and somehow the energy was blocked, preventing a slaying from taking place.

He also saw that the attitude of the group was equally important. When people had been present who were definitely negative to the experience, it had happened to few individuals. But in a group that was highly receptive the gift seemed to pass from one person to another. Sometimes the atmosphere had been so charged that confusion, almost pandemonium, resulted. The idea of suggestibility kept coming to mind. In addition it became more and more clear to him that slaying in the spirit did not inevitably bring release and joy and a new spirit of life and growth. There were some people who found it terrifying and had mostly bad reactions to it. There were those who had come back again and again for the same experience with no apparent change other than a momentary high. He also recalled his mixed feelings as he had watched one evangelist use the experience to take a group of teenagers alternately through terror and bliss. He began to doubt the wisdom of some who proclaimed to the world that slaying in the spirit was their special ministry.

As he began to realize the full extent of psychic influences on these experiences, something within him—something he had not even known was there—said *no* to this ministry and the slayings stopped happening around him. He did not drop matters there, however. This priest had become even more aware of people's need for religious experience, and he went right on studying and trying to understand the place of slaying in the spirit in our religious tradition. In a similar spirit let us turn now to consider the history of this kind of religious happening.

Trance or Ecstasy in Religious History

There are examples all through religious history, including our Christian history, of men and women who encountered such powerful experiences of the divine or the numinous that they seemed to become unconscious of everything around them, sometimes falling to the ground as if in a faint. While we cannot, of course, go back into history and question these individuals, it appears that many of them experienced a state of consciousness remarkably similar to that of slaying. There are similar descriptions of a deep sense of peace and some kind of contact with the divine in this state which has been known as *trance*, religious *ecstasy*, or *rapture*.

The English word trance, which sometimes implies loss of consciousness, comes from Latin and French words meaning "passage" or "to pass from one state to another," from which we also derive the words transit and transition. It also means "to pass away" and so by inference to die, and thus is related to slaying. Our word ecstasy describes a similar experience but usually without loss of consciousness or conscious control. It comes from a Greek term meaning "to stand aside" or "to be knocked down from one's senses." In the latter sense it carries something of the connotation of slaying. Rapture—which conveys the idea of being seized by a state of consciousness other than the ordinary space-time world—is derived from a Latin word meaning "to seize" or "transport." In addition to the modern term slaying in the spirit, there are also Hebrew and Greek words which simply mean "to fall down," which are used in the Bible to describe much the same experiences as these. Another interesting linguistic comparison is from Latin. "Numen," from which the word numinous (the awe-inspiring holy) is derived, has both the meaning of "divine" and also the mean ing "nod." Apparently, a close relation was seen between experiences of the divine and nodding.

It was probably in a state of trance or ecstasy, reached through meditation, that the Gautama Buddha found the enlightenment that started him on his religious way. It also appears that much of the Koran came to Mohammed in such a state, undoubtedly starting with an experience that came out of ordinary sleep. In other cases these experiences happened through rituals, sometimes involving drugs, or they came to individuals autonomously and even out of the blue.

It is very difficult, of course, to make exact comparisons between these experiences from many cultures and different times. We have enough trouble trying to get an adequate picture of religious experience in our own time. When it happens to people who try to describe in our own language what occurs within them, words are still misinterpreted and misunderstood. When the descriptions come from peoples whose languages and points of view may be quite different from our own, and sometimes only from outside observers, we can only point to certain similarities and differences. These happenings in the past (in which individuals lose either contact with the physical world or control over their actions in it, thus, it is often believed, opening themselves to another dimension of reality) have a relation to slaying in the spirit. In some ways what happens may be much the same; in other ways it may be quite different.

These experiences are so numerous and they have so much religious significance that a full-scale study of them is needed. Our purpose is more limited, however. In order to see how deeply these experiences are rooted in the history of religion, particularly our own, we shall look first at some of the examples from primitive religions which are accessible and have been studied carefully. Then we shall consider more fully the experiences found in the Bible and later church history.

One of the most detailed descriptions of this kind of experience is found in Mircea Eliade's scholarly and thought-provoking study, *Shamanism*. With step by step documentation Eliade shows that while shamanism is not the only form of religious ecstasy, this approach to another state of consciousness is found among practically all primitive peoples in all parts of the world. The vocation of shaman undoubtedly comes from the very early history of our religions.

The essence of this vocation lies in an ability to go into a trance state, and then to come back from it bringing knowledge of another world which can be used to restore and heal those who need help. As Eliade remarks,

[In places where] the ecstatic experience is considered the religious experience par excellence, the shaman, and he alone, is the great master of ecstasy. A first definition of this complex phenomenon, and perhaps the least hazardous, will be: shamanism = *technique of ecstasy*. . . . [And, pointing out the difference between shamans and other primitive healers or medicine men,] the shaman specializes in a trance during which his soul is believed to leave his body and ascend to the sky or descend to the underworld.[9]

The ability to go into trance, ecstasy, rapture—whatever one wishes to call it—is one factor which enables the shaman to practice his profession. As in a slaying he lies on the ground immobile, unable to hear or communicate if he is spoken to. When the experience comes unexpectedly, he falls to the ground and lies there in a trance. It is interesting that in many primitive cultures epileptics were considered holy persons, religiously significant just because of their proneness to such seizures of unconsciousness. Epilepsy was even known as the "holy sickness."

Dancing offers another access to the trance state in primitive religions. Most primitive dancing is a religious expression in itself, and there are reports of certain dance rituals in which participants often fall down as if unconscious and then get up in a trance to perform actions which consummate the ritual. In rituals of this kind the dancers often appear to be seized by a group spirit so that they move almost as one person. This is true in Balinese dance. As De Zoete and Spies describe in *Dance and Drama in Bali*, in this trance state even girls who have not been trained perform the most intricate dance patterns. In many cultures drugs are ingested to induce such a state in which a person becomes more attuned to the psychoid world. In *The Wizard of the Upper Amazon* Manuel Cordova-Rios and F. Bruce Lamb give a fascinating account of one such culture.

The kind of "psychic" healings that are being studied among certain less sophisticated peoples today also give evidence of the importance of trance states among primitive groups. John G. Fuller's *Arigo: Surgeon of the Rusty Knife* and David St. Clair's *Drum and Candle* both show that such healings generally take place with the healer in a state of trance or religious ecstasy.

The primitive practices, however, seem a far cry from most modern ideas of religion. In approaching our own tradition it will be helpful to understand something of the relation of different peoples to different states of consciousness. It is not easy for people to attain conscious control and conscious individuality. This comes with ego consciousness which developed late in the history of humankind, as Erich Neumann has pointed out in *The Origins and History of Consciousness*. Primitive men and women are almost more part of the group than they are individuals. They are united by *participation mystique* with others in the group, and they find it very difficult to stand by themselves as separate and autonomous individuals. At a significant ritual like the dances of Bali or the Hopi snake dance one can almost watch the participants merge into the being of the group, allowing the burden of individuality to be taken over by the collective psyche.

In Eastern cultures the same thing can happen without any dramatic experiences to mark the passage from one state to the other. In these cultures there is simply not much concern with the value of individual consciousness, as Joseph Campbell shows in *Myths To Live By*. Eastern religions consider that life in the here and now has only transitory meaning. The individual is merely a momentary expression of an eternal principle, which offers little incentive for the kind of conscious development known in Christian cultures. After all is over and one has been absorbed, perhaps again and again, into this passing pattern of existence, the ultimate goal is to merge once more and lose oneself finally in the vast pool of cosmic consciousness. No wonder it is easy for people in the East to slip into another state of consciousness, scarcely even aware of turning away from one reality toward a psychic or spiritual dimension. In India, for instance, one sees people who seem to dream while they are awake.

In countries that have been deeply influenced by the teach'-
ing of Jesus Christ a different value is placed on individuality and
personal development. Individuals are valued for themselves and
their responsibility to develop their own ego strength has been
cultivated. The trouble is that, beginning with Descartes, thinkers in Western Europe began to go overboard. In their effort to
provide perfectly clear consciousness and control over one's actions and personality, they forgot that there is an eternal, primal
reality which is necessary for individual growth. Ego consciousness became the only reality most Westerners could reach, and
they were cut off from their psychic roots. As C. G. Jung and
other students of our time have seen, our present-day society is
suffering the consequences in neurosis and many of the other
troubles of our violent era. For a great many people the ego has
become an intolerable prison from which they are trying to escape.

It is easy to ignore the fact that one can break out of this
domination by the ego in either positive or negative ways. Many
people seek to escape by becoming part of a group so that their
separation from others no longer feels like a straitjacket. Too
often, however, the lowest common denominator of a group
emerges as its standard and mob instinct takes over for the ego,
robbing the individual of the power to choose his own course of
action. The kinds of impulses that can take possession of a lynch
mob or street gang, or people in time of war, are only extreme
examples of what can happen when the group is allowed to take
control.

Religion, of course, does provide positive ways of re-
establishing contact with realities which are necessary to the ego
and to the whole personality. But we must not forget that even
religious groups can become possessed by destructive ideas and
impulses. Practices like the human sacrifices of the Aztecs, the
Hindu suttee, and the child sacrifices among certain African
tribes have been replaced by more subtle ways of taking out our
destructive reactions on ourselves and those around us. Modern
Christians are certainly not free of these reactions, and it is wise
not to accept every religious expression at face value without

asking what effect there may be on human lives and human actions.

Religious experience has the effect of relaxing the tight control of the ego, opening our personalities to new areas of reality. One way this happens is through experiences of trance and ecstasy. Slaying in the spirit is one variety of such experience. Like tongue speaking, it is an outer expression of an inner state, one that is particularly convincing to people in our materialistic ego-dominated society. Slaying in the spirit leaves no question that something has happened within the individual. Neither the bystander nor the person involved can deny that something very different from ordinary ego consciousness is at work. Are there, then, any precedents for such experience in the history of our own religion?

Biblical Parallels

As we turn to the very early records of our religion, it is important to emphasize again the difficulty of comparing religious experiences today with those in the past. Religious descriptions do not always tell us what was happening inside the person, and this makes it hard to be sure about a complex experience like slaying in the spirit. There was obviously nothing in biblical times exactly similar to a modern service in which people come forward, are touched and fall down; on the other hand, there are many references in the Old and New Testaments to people who fell before God and seemed to be struck down by his spirit.

The words used most frequently in the Bible to speak of such experiences are *naphal* in Hebrew and *piptō* (and several variations) in Greek. These were ordinary words for *falling* which could refer to the natural fall of an object or to an individual being felled by an enemy in battle, or even to falling from favor or grace. They are interesting because of three basic religious meanings which are sometimes difficult to distinguish.

First, people who encountered God sometimes *fell down* before him because they were overcome by his numinous presence, and in some instances the experience was followed by visions.

Falling down before God in this way seems to have been very close to the natural ecstasy reported by many of the mystics and saints, and also similar to what is experienced in slaying in the spirit. This sense of being overpowered by God may also be the symbolic meaning underlying Jesus' falling to the ground in the garden of Gethsemane.

Second, there were times when people *fell to the ground* before God—or in many cultures before another human being of great power and majesty—simply because it was appropriate to prostrate oneself in obeisance. In this case the act was done consciously because it was the required or right thing to do. When the Bible says that someone fell down before God, however, it is often impossible to tell whether this was a conscious act of adoration or whether the person had abandoned himself to God's power and was struck down. Finally, there are several passages describing how either a deep sleep or the spirit of the Lord *fell upon* someone and a vision then came to that person. Some of these instances probably imply that the person also fell to the ground under the power of God's spirit. The biblical text simply does not fill in every detail. One thing is certain, however; evidence is given all through the Bible that people met the divine and responded by falling to the ground. This was one appropriate response to the divine, whether one controlled the action or not.

Abraham responded in this way. When he first received God's promise, a deep sleep fell upon him and he was given the great revelation symbolizing the ritual of covenant, a vision of God as a firebrand passing between the pieces of a sacrifice (Gen. 15:12-21). Later Abraham twice fell upon his face before Yahweh who had appeared to tell him that Sarah would bear him a son in their old age (Gen. 17:3, 17). Moses—who was the great exception in his relations with God—did not fall down before the burning bush, but hid his face; later he told of falling before God after smashing the ten commandments (Ex. 3:6; Deut. 9:18, 25). When Aaron had become priest and performed the sacrifices, the glory of God appeared to the people and they shouted for joy and fell on their faces (Lev. 9:24). Others—Joshua, Manoah and his wife, those who saw Elijah bring down the fire of the Lord, David—each fell to the ground overcome before messengers of God (Jos. 5:14; Jgs. 13:20; 1 Kgs. 18:39; 1 Chr. 21:16).

One of the most interesting descriptions is found in Balaam's speech after the spirit of God came upon him. Balaam said that he had fallen down, but with his eyes wide open, and he went on to tell what God had shown him. Apparently the word *naphal* is used here to mean falling into a condition, probably a trance, in which he could act only as a mouthpiece for the Lord (Num. 24:4, 16). The prophet Ezekiel told how he was overwhelmed by the presence of the Lord and fell upon his face, and how he was then lifted up and given instructions and prophetic visions (Ez. 1:28; 3:23; 43:3; 44:4). When Daniel was trying to understand the meaning of his second vision, one came to him who was apparently an angel. Daniel fell to the ground senseless and was then lifted up and instructed about the vision (Dan. 8:15-26). In the Book of Job there are references to the visions and dreams which warn and instruct people when deep sleep falls upon them. Job also reminds his visitors that when they come to face God, dread of him may fall upon them (Jb. 4:13; 33:15; 13:11).

These passages certainly show that falling down before the Lord was an honored and not infrequent happening or custom. Sometimes the text makes it clear that the act of falling was involuntary, resulting from the kind of openness that allowed the prophet to let go and lie prostrate while exploring new areas of consciousness. When a person was really seeking direct contact with the Lord, one way of consciously preparing to face God was simply to fall down before him.

Essentially the same tradition is found in the New Testament. The Greek word "to fall" (*piptō* and the variations formed by adding different prefixes) has just as many ambiguous meanings as either the Hebrew or English words, and it was used just as often to signify the religious meanings outlined above. All through the gospels, beginning with the formal obeisance of the wise men in Matthew 2:11, people fell down before Jesus.

Peter fell down in awe at what happened when the fishermen followed Jesus' instructions (Lk. 5:8). The woman who touched Jesus' robe and was healed fell down before him, as the leper also did who came back to thank him (Mk. 5:33; Lk. 8:47; 17:16). Jairus fell at Jesus' feet to ask help for his daughter, and the Syro-Phoenician woman did the same thing, while a leper fell down before him to ask for his own healing, and Mary to ask why Jesus had not come to help her brother Lazarus (Mk. 5:22; 7:25; Lk. 8:41; 5:12; Jn. 11:32). Apparently those with unclean spirits often fell down before him, crying out that he was the Son of God (Mk. 3:11). This was the immediate reaction of the Gerasene demoniac, and also of the epileptic boy who was tormented by a spirit (Lk. 8:28; Mk. 9:20).

Confronted with the overwhelming experience of Jesus' transfiguration and hearing a voice speak from heaven, the three disciples fell to the ground on their faces in great fear. It even appeared to Luke that sleep had fallen upon them (Mt. 17:6; Lk. 9:32). In the garden of Gethsemane when the soldiers came to arrest Jesus and he told them that he was the one they were looking for, the armed men fell backward and dropped to the ground (Jn. 18:6). This certainly did not happen as a conscious act of reverence. Faced by an angel, the guards at the empty tomb were also struck down and became like dead men, of course falling to the ground (Mt. 28:4).

The same kind of thing was also recorded in the book of Acts. The most notable occurrence in this period was Paul's experience of falling to the ground before a light flashing from heaven and hearing a voice, identified as Jesus', telling him what to do (Acts 9:3-6). Twice more the story is repeated in Paul's own words (22:6-10; 26:12-16), and in 2 Corinthians 12:1-5 he speaks of just such an experience of revelation which had occurred fourteen years before. While we cannot be sure whether Paul was referring to the experience described in Acts or to some other, his words suggest that there is probably a very real connection between visions and falling down before the Lord. In his first letter to the Corinthians Paul had already emphasized the importance of falling down in worship of the Lord (1 Cor. 14:25).

When Peter preached in the home of Cornelius, a large group were gathered to hear him, and the Holy Spirit fell upon all of them (Acts 10:44-46; 11:15). Considering Peter's trance and the visions which had made this gathering possible, it would have been very surprising if some of them had not also fallen to the floor. The book of Revelation itself is testimony to this understanding of the relation of worship to a prophetic state of consciousness. John fell down as if dead before a vision of the Son of God and immediately was raised up to write down what he saw and heard (Rev. 1:17). He told again and again how the "elders" fell down to worship God (Rev. 4:10; 5:14; 7:11; 11:16; 19:4), but this, John learned, was for God alone. Twice he fell down before angels and was instructed that even angels should not be worshiped in this way (Rev. 19:10, 22:8-9).

As Acts shows, the new church also experienced some unpleasant fallings. The sorcerer Bar-Jesus tried to keep Paul from converting the governor of one island, and at Paul's bidding a mist and darkness fell upon Bar-Jesus and he was blind (Acts 13:11). When a deep sleep fell upon Eutychus, this led to a greater fall. The boy fell from an upper window and was only revived by Paul's intervention (Acts 20:8-10). Finally there was the tragic fall of Ananias and Sapphira which reveals a less attractive aspect of the early church. This couple lied to the fellowship about their property, and when Peter questioned each of them, they fell down dead (Acts 5:1-10).

From this look at the biblical record, we can see quite clearly that falling down before the Lord was a fairly common phenomenon. It was associated with awe and holy fear. This seemed to be the natural reaction to Jesus when his numinous power was revealed. People do tremble and falter before the full impact of the divine, just as the three disciples did at the transfiguration, or like all of the followers who were filled with awe and fear on the way to Jerusalem in Mark 10:32. Falling down—whether it comes mainly from unconscious psychophysical causes, or from conscious adoration, or from a mixture of the two—seems to be a natural way of expressing this overwhelming awe. Very probably religious swooning occurred occasionally in enthusiastic groups like the one at Corinth, along with other evidences of being filled with the spirit of God.

Evidences of "Slaying" in Later Church History

By the time the New Testament was set in the form we know it today, the church was moving away from enthusiastic expression. The writers of that time show a clear desire to present the sensible and rational side of Christianity. After all, the church was fighting to stay alive within the Empire and it could not afford to appear strange or outlandish. Beginning in the second century, as I have traced in my book *Tongue Speaking*, there was a real effort to play down this kind of outer expression of the inner Christian experience. There are enough indications in the writings to show that expressions like tongue speaking, and probably trance and ecstasy, did occur—perhaps on emotionally packed occasions such as the Easter baptisms. But this was not the kind of thing that was being emphasized by the church.

Then about the year 175 these enthusiastic expressions became associated with the heresy of Montanism. Montanus, who obviously let charismatic gifts carry him and his followers off the track, was described by the historian Eusebius in this way:

> . . . there would be sudden seizure, he would fall into a trance, and start raving in his speech. He would speak with strange tongues, too, and prophesy (or so it was called) in a manner quite contrary to that which has come down to us, by continuous tradition, from earlier times.[10]

The very fact that the church classed this behavior as heretical drove it still further underground. When Christianity became the established religion of the Empire under Constantine, imperial weight was added to moral authority to suppress these experiences still more. They continued to happen in the monastic orders which grew up when the church began to adapt to the ways of the world. But inside or outside the cloister, these experiences were not really recognized, and enthusiasm—which literally means "being inspired by God's spirit"—was left to take its own course.

Ronald Knox's book *Enthusiasm* presents a detailed history of the more direct and visible manifestations in the Middle Ages and later on. While Knox writes somewhat sarcastically and from a particular bias, most of the facts are included. He describes a "nether" world of medieval heresy in which there were sometimes outer expressions of great spiritual intensity. He does omit witchcraft, however, and Jeffrey Russell's study *Witchcraft in the Middle Ages* is an excellent source if one is trying to understand all the kinds of possession by demonic forces, the seizures and falling down which were not exactly uncommon almost into modern times.

Among the Montanists there was a belief that people can achieve complete freedom from sin and also that Christ's thousand-year reign on earth was about to begin. These beliefs have often gone hand in hand with trance experiences attributed to the Holy Spirit. Knox quotes descriptions of several such sects, among them a fourteenth-century group in Flanders who danced until they fell to the ground and then told of ecstatic visions which they said came from the Holy Spirit. The same beliefs and similar experiences, with more or less order, occurred among great numbers of Anabaptists. They were described by an early observer:

> When under the influence of the Spirit, their countenances were contorted, they made deprecatory gestures, fell on the ground as if in a fit, and finally lay stretched out as if they were dead. . . .[11]

After this there were similar experiences among the Jansenists and Quietists. The Protestant Camisards in southern France became known around the world for their prophetic utterances when they fell down in trance, almost unconscious. The Quakers in England were persecuted, partly for their "unseemly behavior" when they fell in trance or ecstasy, and in America the same things were described as common experiences among the Shakers.

The influences of the Methodists grew by leaps and bounds as Wesley was able to use these experiences to help people change their lives. It was undoubtedly Wesley's influence that changed Britain from a nation of dissolute, gin-drinking failures into a power capable of resisting Napoleon's drive to make Europe his own empire. The same influence was felt on the American frontier all through the last century in the camp meetings that carried these experiences out to the new settlers along with our westward movement. The history of religious practice, from the earliest shamans to modern Pentecostalism, shows that there has been hardly a period in which such psycho-physical experiences were not present in some degree.

A Theory of Personality

In trying to approach these experiences we are dealing with people's consciousness and mental processes, and this is one of the most difficult elements of our world to understand or explain. We are so close to our own experiences and to the way they give us consciousness that we either forget about the processes that are going on in our minds, or else we assume that we understand all about them. Yet the greatest students of the mind suggest only tentative theories. Arthur Lovejoy, for instance, concluded his brilliant study of the theories, *The Revolt Against Dualism*, by telling a myth in the Platonic fashion, saying that this was the closest he could come to explaining our conscious knowing.

Our inability to explain how we *get* consciousness makes it very difficult to understand how consciousness is *lost*. What does happen in sleep, for example, when consciousness ceases its ordinary activity and relinquishes control? Sleep can be described as a change in brain waves, but how it happens and what causes it are simply not known, and there are not even many theories about how it works. The same thing is true of hypnosis. This is another common experience which can be observed by anyone who wishes to, but it is no better understood than sleep. We solve nothing by describing experiences like slaying as hysteria due to hypnotic suggestion, or in terms of sudden sleep. This is simply describing one unknown by another. In fact, hypnosis comes from the Greek word for sleep and means a condition like normal sleep.

If we are to make some sense of these experiences, we must have a theory of personality which accounts for various human states, both conscious and unconscious, those under our control and those which are not. One problem in understanding and evaluating psycho-physical experiences is the prejudice that our minds consist only of conscious components and that we are in touch only with physical reality. What I propose is another view, which is also the Christian view, and which I have described at some length in my books *Encounter with God* and *The Other Side of Silence*. It is similar in many ways to the view of Plato, and in modern times to those of Sigmund Freud and C. G. Jung. It is offered as a theory or hypothesis, not as a final answer. It is an attempt to provide a model which will help us see what is happening in these experiences which we have found so common in certain religious circles.

Let us consider the idea that the human psyche or mind or personality is larger than we sometimes think and that it contains unconscious elements as well as conscious ones. Let us also try to see that we are in touch with two different realities—one that comes to us through sense experience, and one which is revealed by intuition and imagination—and that this second reality includes not only the psyche itself but also a world of realities that are similar to the psyche but outside of it. At this point a diagram may help to clarify this complex view of our personalities.

The two experiences of reality are suggested by dividing the diagram by a line down the middle, with the psyche (the small triangle) poking its tip of consciousness into the world of physical experiences on the right. These experiences are not diagrammed since we are all aware of them. We have considerable control over them although, as shown by T. S. Kuhn in *The Structure of Scientific Revolutions* and other students, our expectations (often unconscious assumptions) determine much of what we see in the physical world.

We have very little control, however, over experiences that come from the unconscious (on the left). Our slips of the tongue, mistakes, neuroses often arise in the unconscious. Here we find forgotten personal experiences which can rise up to haunt us. We are all affected by powerful universal patterns of experience or archetypes which determine much of our behavior—for instance, our attitude toward the opposite sex, toward mothering, or being mothered, toward authority. These forces can present a light and wholesome side or, especially when they operate completely unconsciously, a dark and demonic side. Finally there are the two great irreducible forces of the Self and the destructive tendencies or the Evil One, which can work in and through us, or can enter the physical world directly and work around us.

A Model or Scheme

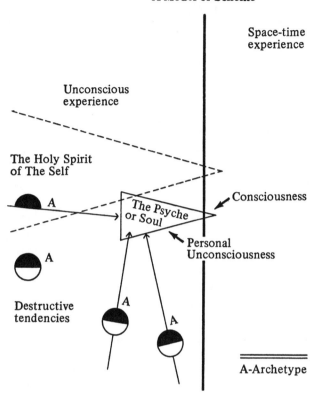

The importance of knowing this world of unconscious experience seems obvious. Yet there are various ways of encountering it, and as George Maloney suggests, the church is very aware of the dangers. Fr. Maloney writes:

> [The church] knows the power of hysteria and of self-induced psychic phenomena once the conscious control has yielded to an opening of one's unconscious through mental illness or prolonged introspection as a part of the pursuit of holiness. It also knows the power of demonic forces to communicate and even gain control over certain physical and psychic areas of a human life.[12]

The church uses discernment. As Fr. Maloney points out, St.

Gemman Galgani was canonized by Pius XII in spite of certain neurotic tendencies that produced psychic experiences which had little to do with her sanctity. Let us see some of the ways people contact these unconscious elements, and then consider one of them—the way of hypnotic trance—a little further.

These elements, of course, can emerge spontaneously, and this happens most commonly in dreams. It can also happen through falling in love, as well as once in a while through visions, ESP experiences, or even automatic writing. Experiences such as healing, tongue speaking and prophecy, the stigmata, and slaying in the spirit can also come without being sought, bringing unexpected contact with realities that are usually unconscious. Then there are ways of seeking encounter with these realities consciously because individuals wish to find such contact.

One way is to open one's conscious mind to the unconscious by meditative techniques, through religious ritual, or by recording and interpreting one's dreams and visions and learning to work consciously with elements from the unconscious. Active imagination, phantasy, contemplating the realities opened up by religious myths, painting and other artistic expressions all give access to the unconscious and help in developing this kind of contact.

A second way is through auto-suggestion, which involves a carefully structured approach to the unconscious by the kind of programmed, positive thinking described by Claude Bristol in *The Magic of Believing*. Much of New Thought and Science of Mind is based on such an approach. Third, individuals can open themselves by taking various hallucinogenic drugs, or by inviting one kind of spirit or another to possess them as mediums do, or by using an ouija board or automatic writing. Finally one can become open to experiences of the unconscious by submitting to hypnosis or falling under the suggestive power of an individual or a group.

A Word about Hypnosis

Ever since Mesmer's discovery of hypnosis was finally accepted in the nineteenth century, this kind of "sleep" has been studied by one group after another. Through hypnosis one person seems to gain control of another's unconscious mind and be able to manipulate it so that the hypnotized individual is then able to do many things that are usually impossible. Memories buried beyond recall can be described in minute detail; pain can be anesthetized, memories right at hand can be selectively erased, and physical feats ordinarily impossible can be performed. The control of bodily functions, such as heart rate, oxygen consumption, etc., which bio-feedback techniques have only begun to offer, can be provided almost instantaneously under hypnosis. Through this apparent mobilization of the unconscious mind by an outside agent, any of the physical effects we have found among various religious groups can be duplicated. Certainly getting a person in hypnotic trance to fall to the floor would be a simple hypnotic procedure.

William Sargant in *Battle for the Mind* and Jerome Frank in *Persuasion and Healing* discuss the relation of hypnotism, suggestion, and methods of thought control to religious conversion and healing, and belief in general. Both show that suggestion plays a part in these religious experiences. Sargant also shows that many confessions are wrung from innocent people who are suggestible and can be persuaded to agree with what is suggested, even to confessing murder. The more conventional a person, the more suggestible he is and the more easily hypnotized. In fact living a purely conventional life is a sort of group hypnotism itself. We are far more open to the suggestions of those around us than we sometimes think.

Studies of brainwashing in communist countries and in Korea after our involvement there show the way ordinary people may be induced to profess something quite contrary to their real character, and believe it. Brainwashing is not just a police method. It is a fact of life whenever people's emotions and their hopes and expectations become involved. Anyone with a charismatic personality will have power to suggest beliefs and behavior to many people. On the other hand, wise use of suggestion can open people to themselves and help them follow their own path. In our human interactions we will be using suggestion whether we like it or not. The important thing is to realize that we are using it, and to be as careful as possible about our motives so that we help people move toward growth and autonomy rather than dependence and stagnation.

There is no sharp line between our induction into conventional society by parents, teachers and peers and the more direct kind of suggestion which can dominate a whole group, often in a very primitive and atavistic way. Sometimes a group spirit seems to seize an individual and use him so that he becomes little more than a puppet of the mob spirit. C. G. Jung has described Hitler as such a puppet in *Civilization in Transition*. Again, there is no sharp line between this kind of suggestion and hypnosis. Similar results can be achieved through each of these ways of suggestion. In addition, nearly all of the religious psycho-physical states we have considered can be experienced through hypnosis or suggestion.

The problem for us Westerners is that it is difficult for vital religious experience to reach us. We have been suggested into the idea that we live in a purely space-time universe and that there is nothing else for us to experience. One reason for the use of marijuana by modern youth, as Andrew Weil has suggested, is that it is an "activated placebo" which gives a legitimate excuse to experience a wider spectrum of reality. Western rational materialism does not allow for any reality to break through which could give us religious experiences, and it does not suggest any way.

In his book *Masters of the Heart* Andrew Canale has described the work of T. X. Barber with whom he worked. Professor Barber, he writes, has given telling evidence that

> . . . a person's attitudes, motivations and expectations and the experimental setting are such crucial aspects of "hypnosis" that to postulate a separate "hypnotic state" may be misleading. In other words, the mental set of the subject and the experimental conditions rather than an imposed state of hypnosis are mainly responsible for the inner experiences of "hypnotized" subjects in this view. He has gone further to show that subjects who score well while under "hypnosis" will score as well, or will experience the suggestions as well, when not under hypnosis. Openness to the realm to which "hypnosis" purportedly admits one can be sufficient entry fee to that realm without undergoing hypnosis.[13]

Hypnosis, in reality, is only an extreme form of suggestion to which we are all subject to some degree. The question is not whether we are open to suggestion, but what kind. Does the suggestion we are accepting lead to wider and more fruitful experience, to growth and the wholeness of personality which Christianity demands of us? The world today offers various choices. We can follow the suggestion of materialistic behaviorism which leads to Walden Two, that of Sartre and existentialism which leads to a "no exit" sign and nausea, or that of TM which leads to absorption into cosmic mind. Or we can seek the suggestion of Christian ritual and Christian experience, which lead to the creative center of reality, to Jesus, the risen Christ. This also offers safeguards against being demolished while seeking this divine center of Love.

The Source of Psycho-Physical Experiences

The next and perhaps most basic consideration is to see what causes such experiences as slaying in the spirit. Here a simplistic answer simply will not do. It is easy to describe tongue speaking, for instance, as a gift of the spirit and stop there. But to understand the value of tongue speaking one must not only compare it with other gifts such as knowledge, wisdom, healing, and so on, but try to understand its effect on individuals and see why it happens to certain people, or at certain times to groups of people almost indiscriminately.

In one way or another the gifts are all psycho-physical experiences. They all have some kind of visible, outer effect which shows that something spiritual (or at least non-physical) is at work. It is important to get an idea of the possible causes and see their relation to the effects. In the case of tongue speaking and slaying in the spirit this does not mean deciding beforehand that certain instances all come from the Holy Spirit, while others are all the result of either hypnotic suggestion or something demonic. In fact, it appears that these psycho-physical manifestations can arise from seven different sources, and this is probably the reason Christian writers have been so cautious in encouraging them. In considering the following list of causes, it will be helpful to remember the previous diagram of our various kinds of experiences, realizing that more than one factor may be at work at the same time to produce a certain result.

1. The immediate preparation for the psycho-physical state may come as a direct suggestion by the individual to his own unconscious, which is thus self-mobilized and proceeds to produce the desired results. This is auto-suggestion. The experience can also be fraudulently reported or even consciously imitated, but this is quite different from auto-suggestion.

2. The experience can be brought about by the suggestion of a group (remembering that this is not necessarily a negative statement). Thus group expectations may aid in the release of outer physical manifestations like tongue speaking or trance or healing.

3. The experience can be induced by ordinary hypnosis. The variety of physical effects which can be created in this way is practically limitless. Wounds like the stigmata have been suggested through hypnosis. The most common and observable of all the effects is hypnotic sleep in which the person slumps in his chair and yet—like slaying in the spirit—can recall all that went on during the experiment when asked.

4. The experience may arise autonomously in the same way that dreams arise, coming from the part of the psyche shown on the left in the diagram, from the personal unconscious or from the deeper recesses of the psyche. Likewise when there is real inner stress, many people do faint or drop to the floor.

5. As the diagram and the hypothesis I have presented suggest, there is a realm of reality outside our psyches—represented by the archetypes in the diagram—which can trigger or induce these psycho-physical experiences. Very much as mediums (at least purportedly) allow themselves to be used by some autonomous reality beyond the individual psyche, a person may become possessed or be triggered into a psycho-physical manifestation by some disembodied spirit or non-physical reality with both light and dark sides.

6. As the evidence strongly indicates, there is a destructive aspect of reality which can possess and use human beings, and can initiate these experiences, as well as most of the states and graces that come from God himself. Charles Williams' novel

Shadows of Ecstasy is a dramatic exposition of this possibility.

7. And last of all there is the possibility that these psycho-physical manifestations may actually be evidence of the intervention or influence or action of God, his Holy Spirit, or one of his emissaries or angelic powers.

Unquestionably caution and discrimination are needed in approaching these experiences. To encourage them in every case uncritically as manifestations of the divine would probably be just as dangerous as trying to suppress them entirely or making fun of them. Those who get into this area need wisdom, cautious discernment, and knowledge of the human psyche and its pathological states, as well as knowledge of God and his Spirit, and an abundance of charity. This appears to apply to all the gifts of the spirit, all the psycho-physical religious manifestations, as well as slaying in the spirit, since any of them can apparently arise from many different levels.

Many people discredit an experience like going down under the power purely because of its emotionalism. Studies of the mechanics of conversion, however, show that it may be necessary for people to be under considerable emotional stress in order to make any basic change in their ways of acting and reacting. Pavlov learned accidentally what severe stress could do to animal behavior. He was studying the amount of stress it took to make a dog switch a previously conditioned response—to love a hated master, for instance, or avoid something previously desired—when the 1924 Leningrad flood occurred and a group of dogs were nearly drowned. The switch in their reaction patterns was so dramatic that Pavlov, after further study, was forced to conclude that every creature has a point at which stress will change ingrained reactions and behavior which nothing else can touch.

Since human beings may need emotional stress and upheaval so as to make an about-face and be "converted," we should be very careful about our attitude toward the release of emotions in experiences like slaying in the spirit. Such emotionalism may provide the necessary psycho-physical preparation for openness to God and his spirit. At the same time, we must also remember that this process can be used for brainwashing as well as for actual conversion.

Whether or not a person loses consciousness in slaying

probably depends on how much one wishes to remember. In the latest studies of sleep it is shown that whenever a person is awakened from sleep some kind of mental activity is found going on. Usually we forget it and think that we have been totally unconscious. The same thing is apparently true of people who are revived after being clinically dead. In his book *Life After Life* Raymond A. Moody reports his study of a number of such cases, revealing the dramatic fact that there was no loss of consciousness. Although in each case the body was totally inert, unresponsive to stimuli, and so "dead," the person often heard what was going on and could report how his body looked and what was being done to revive it. What is called loss of consciousness seems to be only a failure to remember what one has been experiencing. Whether a person remembers all that goes on in a slaying is probably not very important so long as the experience results in the kind of openness that can bring transformation. How, then, can the church help people who experience slaying in the spirit find the possible dividends?

Pastoral Considerations

My first pastoral suggestion is a general one. The individuals involved in ministering slaying in the spirit should be as aware, as clearly conscious as possible, of their own motivations in encouraging these experiences. In *The Christian and the Supernatural* I have suggested eight dangers which face people who use ESP abilities. The same dangers may be met by individuals who have the capacity to induce or minister any dramatic psycho-physical experience. These pitfalls are:

1. Using this capacity for personal prestige or power, influence or profit.

2. Using this capacity in a way which could hurt another person or damage anyone psychologically.

3. Letting fraud or deceit creep into the use of this capacity, for instance by pretending to be more of an instrument than one knows is true.

4. Encouraging this experience by other than natural methods, by using individual or group pressure, or by continu-

ing meetings late into the night so that people become exhausted and more open to suggestion and direct influence.

5. Either thinking that one is dealing with a power which comes only from God, or believing that one is strong enough to control any other forces encountered in the spiritual world.

6. Encouraging the experience just for itself, rather than because it can lead to a deeper and fuller Christian life.

7. Using such a dramatic capacity to lord it over people, to dominate them either consciously or unconsciously. Any religious capacity can become destructive if it is used to keep people in subjection to authority.

8. Judging or looking down on people who do not receive this experience and considering them inferior to those who have received it.

Once the dangers have been honestly faced, there are ways of testing one's use of this ministry. The best test I have found is to ask oneself the following questions:

Does my expression of this ministry spring out of love?

Does it come from the kind of love which wants me to know the world and human beings as they are, and tries to help me accept myself, the world, and other people in this way?

Does it result in an increase of this love, promoting psychological, intellectual and spiritual growth, both in myself and others?

Can I see healing effects on individuals—body, mind and soul—and in strengthening and building up the group through this experience?

Is there an increase of hope and faith and joy, and do I see others given courage and liberated to discover their own gifts and talents?

As I have come to know myself well, I have realized how deep and diverse my motives may be and how careful I must be in any ministry I undertake. It is all too easy—and I am not too different from most normal individuals—to find myself ministering to my own power needs, hindering rather than promoting growth. I also have to watch to see that I do not become infected by the collective evil which is so much a part of our broken world.

Finally I have some specific suggestions for using the capacity for slaying in the spirit in the most creative and effective way. First, *the atmosphere and size of the group is important.* The value of this ministry is in opening people to the power of the Holy Spirit. Even in small groups without confusion, we humans have enough trouble hearing what the Spirit wants of us without confusing that voice with the wishes of a large group reinforcing the power of a charismatic leader. As the priest whose story we have told found, there were times when he had to begin the service with people already lying on the floor in the midst of confusion. For nearly everyone slaying in the spirit is most effective when it occurs in the calm atmosphere of a small group, or when a minister is praying privately for one individual. At such times the workings of the Spirit have a chance to move on their own, without being drowned out by the expectations of the crowd.

Second, *the need for pastoral follow-up is even more important.* Slaying in the spirit is an experience of initiation into another realm of being. The Pentecostal churches realized a long time ago that psycho-physical phenomena open people to a variety of influences which can sometimes leave an individual worse off than before. And so they provide close fellowship and support for those new to the experience.

There is just as much reason to treat slaying in the spirit in the same way. If the experience is genuine, the person will be opened to a deep level of the unconscious, and this is not always peaches and cream. Even with the certainty of being opened to God by the Holy Spirit, most people need help to integrate this experience into the total fabric of their lives. One main reason for spiritual direction and discernment is that people do come into contact with elements of spirit, both positive and negative (those on the left side in the diagram on page 39). These are just as real as things in the outer world. There are also real ways of dealing with the world of spirit, and pastors need to work with the deep wisdom of our Christian tradition so as to help people learn these ways, especially after experiencing slaying. Without this kind of pastoral follow-up the results of the experience can be neutral or worse.

Third, *the value of slaying as an initiation and part of a learning program should be stressed, and repeated use discouraged.* The "good feeling" which people sometimes look for over and over again in slaying does not necessarily indicate value. I am reminded of a psychiatrist who was given fifty shock treatments, and they made him feel so good that he gave the same treatment to all of his patients—with disastrous results. Repetition of the experience often means that the individual can be using slaying to avoid problems rather than to solve them and get on with the process of spiritual growth. TM and tranquilizers can be used in this way, and so can hallucinogenic drugs and some forms of thought control. This is a problem for spiritual direction, discernment, and pastoral care, including a wise and compassionate understanding of human personality and our difficulties which can help these individuals develop toward their birthright as sons and daughters of God. There appears to be no easy way to provide spiritual growth. This demands pastoral care and direction.

Fourth, *ways of realizing the content of the experience, the divine encounter, must be provided.* An experience of going down under the power may give just the push that is needed to start an individual—like a car with a dead battery—moving toward growth in the spirit. But to continue growing, a person needs to keep realizing, not the form of the original experience, but the same content in other forms with power to touch new areas of one's imagination and bring growth in new areas of one's life. This is where Oriental and Western mysticism part company. In the East such an encounter is valued because it leads to merging into cosmic mind; in the West one is seeking to meet the Risen Christ and be transformed by him. In the Christian tradition God established our goal when he made humans in his own image and then came as one of them to reveal himself. Imageless experiences fall short of the goal of that encounter. If these psychophysical experiences start a person toward that goal, they are useful, but if they do not, they may even be a hindrance.

Finally, *the test of love must be applied in all that one does to minister or follow up these experiences.* Do they lead the individuals to a deeper knowledge of Jesus Christ, to a deeper desire to allow his Spirit to work in their lives, and to a deeper love of God and man? After all, as William Sargant remarks in discussing the changes that came out of Wesley's meetings, the proof of the pudding is in the eating. Any gift must ultimately be tested by its results.

There is renewed interest in the spiritual dimension in this last quarter of the twentieth century. One aspect of it is the realization that the spiritual domain is real, and that it can affect our bodies as well as our minds and spirits. One manifestation of this new understanding is the ministry of slaying in the spirit. It stands as a symbolic and dramatic giving over of one's conscious control to God, as a symbolic dying and rising again. This should be accompanied by a great sense of reverence. Because this kind of experience touches so deep into the human being, the greatest discernment and delicacy should be used by those ministering in this area. It can have real value when it is used as an entrance to the process of growth in spiritual and moral life. When it becomes separated from this value and from the regular institutional life of the church, and is sought just for the experience itself, slaying in the spirit can divert people from seeking the reality that Christianity offers. It can also cause harm by giving outsiders an inaccurate picture of what is involved in the Christian way. In conclusion slaying in the spirit in my opinion should be given its place and not forbidden, but it should be used only judiciously and with discernment.

Chapter III
The Reality of a Spiritual World:
The Demonic and Angelic Re-Examined

There is not much point in discussing discernment of spirits unless there is a spiritual world to discern. If we are indeed confined to a world of consciousness, space and time, talking about spiritual influences is quite nonsensical. There really is no meaning to the practice of discernment as Paul refers to it in his letter to the Corinthians. If one is going to try to distinguish which influences within a life come from God and which come from some other source, it is first of all necessary to believe that there is a spiritual world and that it affects our world profoundly.

In order to get into the subject of discernment we must give some good reasons for believing that this practice makes sense. In the last two chapters we made a suggestion and an hypothesis that there might be such a reality. Now we must offer the evidence for this contention. In so doing we are running counter to the generally accepted view of most academic biblical study.

One aspect of the New Testament narrative which has been rejected almost universally in modern times is the belief in the realm of spiritual beings, a vast realm of angelic, and also demonic beings. Along with the belief in spiritual healing, dreams, visions and other such intrusions into our self-contained physical world, the idea of active and effective spiritual entities is regarded as absurd. Nineteenth-century liberals merely divided the biblical account, cutting out these unacceptable parts. Bultmann and his followers actively reject them as a contamination of myth which must be removed before modern man can understand the gospel. Barth simply does not discuss them; since

they do not fall within his view of the world, he does not look at
them.

Are spiritual beings merely superstition, concocted out of
whole cloth in human's minds? Are they the pre-scientific imaginings of primitive people, associated with magic? I would suggest that the idea of a spiritual realm of discrete and identifiable
entities is not absurd. It deserves serious consideration today,
quite apart from magic; and it has received such consideration—
sometimes too realistically—in almost every culture and in
every age, with the exception of our own, the culture of Western
Europe and America since the Enlightenment.

The Problem

There are good reasons why enlightened Westerners have
turned away from their belief in a realm of spiritual reality. The
first was probably a reaction to the witch-hunting of the
eighteenth century. The second was the positivism of Comte and
the growing materialism of our time. Probably the foremost reason most people today cannot believe in angels or demons is that
modern Western people have let their ability to know, their idea
of science, mislead them into doubting the existence of any
reality they cannot touch or understand. Non-material reality,
then, cannot exist.

The creed which underlies this point of view can be stated
rather plainly: There is only matter and the laws that govern it.
The psyche is merely an epiphenomenon or an outgrowth or
appendage of matter. With our sense experience we can reach
matter, and with our reason we reach law, but there is no faculty
with which we reach any realm of spiritual reality. Since our
psyche is nothing but a manifestation of matter, it can have no
independent existence, and therefore there can be no spiritual
beings like us. We are unique, just an evolutionary accident, and
not a very important one at that.

The Christians in the midst of this world-view find themselves in a somewhat awkward position. Of course they believe
in matter; this much is legitimate. They also believe in reason,
and so they may believe in a rational and theoretical God who

has made this matter and may influence it through some unknown agency. They may even reach out to this theoretical God, but only in a rational way which does not touch them by experience. The reality of the soul as a living, vital center is therefore very difficult to hang on to. It becomes a metaphysical principle instead of a feeling, experiencing center. Just try to find the reality of a scientific theory with no laboratory or test tubes or Bunsen burners. In much the same way, modern human beings are largely denied real souls; for they cannot admit into their lives any reality which can be touched and experienced independently of their experiences of the material world.

The New Testament Perspective

The New Testament, on the contrary, gives us no such narrow world-view but a very clear picture of two worlds which impinge upon each other. There is a world of matter and also a world of spiritual reality which includes God, the devil, angels, demons, both good and evil (or unclean) spirits, principalities, thrones, powers, dominions, authorities, and beggarly elements. The human being is caught between these two worlds and participates in both of them. This second realm, in which the human being experiences realities equally as important as matter, is met in dreams, visions, and spiritual encounters of various kinds. Even when people are not aware of this world, the beings in it influence them, usually pricking them spitefully with physical or mental illness and sin.

Since one of the prime objects of recent theology has been to eliminate ideas like this from the Christian faith, we are faced quite directly with the question of what we are to do with this aspect of the New Testament. Does it have validity for our time? Does it speak of truth and reality, or is it superstition that ought to be discarded?

Two things seem probable. If all the passages about spiritual entities and the references to them must be removed, this strikes at the validity of the whole gospel narrative and the authority of the evangelists as well. The New Testament then becomes little more than an interesting, although highly elevated, ancient literary document.

Second, if we discard the belief in the reality of spiritual beings, we cut ourselves off from the possibility of real contact with a real God; and we diminish the possibility of believing in a real soul, a vital psyche within ourselves. Indeed, it is the very contact with these archetypal spiritual powers which often gives us the conviction that there lies beyond us a spiritual being too large for us to experience in most instances. As Aquinas held, we know God through the agency of angels. This is also the way we know the reality of our own souls. Our ability to contact this spiritual realm and deal with it is one excellent reason for knowing that our souls belong in essence to the same realm of being and are not just epiphenomenal to matter. To discard belief in a psychic realm, and so in our own souls, would seem to have grave consequences for real religion.

Depth Psychology

Besides this, a study of depth psychology reveals that the understanding of spiritual realities which we find in the New Testament is quite consistent with both good sense and actual experience of any real breadth. It shows, in fact, how much closer the world-view of the New Testament is to the true nature of the world we live in than the rationalistic and materialistic view which begins by ruling these things out as none of its affair and ends with an aside to the audience at large, "Look, we have proved that they don't exist."

All that must be carefully ruled out is the naive belief in demons and angels as material beings which popular fancy concocts. It is the projection of these non-physical contents which is absurd, the concretized angel or demon—the materialized dragon, the witch or werewolf, the gnome—which is ridiculous. In fairy tales we have examples of these things as non-material realities; but the folk legend then goes on to turn the fairy-tale creature into a concrete fact, and in this lies the naiveté. As I have shown in my book, *God, Dreams, and Revelation*,[1] the New Testament is anything but naive; it regards encounters with these realities on the level of visions and dreams as real psychic experiences of a real non-physical world.

Psychic Reality

To describe an experience as psychic is not to say that it is either ephemeral or unreal. There is a realm of psychic reality which is not reducible to physical reality and which does have a profound effect on our bodies as well as our souls. It was experience with this realm that led the New Testament writers to talk about angels, demons and other spirits, and causes psychologists to speak of *autonomous complexes* and *archetypes*. Victor White, a highly educated and able theologian, as well as a man with deep experience in the psychology of Carl Jung, has expressed this in his excellent study of psychology and religion, *God and the Unconscious*. He remarks that the theologian and the psychologist, in talking about these experiences, "each describes an observed occurrence from a different view-point," and that each is referring to the same phenomenon.[2] He also observes:

> In the pages of the New Testament, Satan and the devils may be said to be fairly ubiquitous from the beginning to the end. The polite efforts of nineteenth-century Liberal criticism to exorcise the demons from the New Testament, to explain away its more "devilish" passages as a later and superstitious adulteration of the pure ethical milk of the Gospel, or at least to apologize for them as an unimportant concession to contemporary illusions, have proved a dismal failure. Even the most radical criticism of *Formgeschichte* holds that these passages belong to the most primitive strata, the essential core, of the evangelical tradition. Especially since Schweitzer and Otto, it has become difficult to read the Gospels at all otherwise than as an account of the struggle between the *de jure* Reign of God and the *de facto* Reign of Satan—the actual "prince" or "god" of this world over human hearts, minds and affairs. "The devil," Tertullian will say, with customary exaggeration and insight, "is fully

known only to Christians." The coming of Christ itself
evokes the spirit of anti-Christ; only when the full light
shines in the darkness is the intensity of the darkness made
manifest. Not only the words and actions of Christ as related in the Gospels, but also the Epistles, and still more
obviously the Apocalypse, are largely unintelligible except
on the supposition of the reality and activity of Satan and
other malevolent spirits.[3]

What we wish to do in the following pages is to demonstrate
the truth of this statement. We shall look first at the gospels to
show how widespread and important angels and other spirits
were, in both their positive and negative functioning. We shall
see how Jesus' very view of human personality, and of human
salvation, depends upon his view of these realities. We shall look
then at the rest of the New Testament where we find the same
pervasive conviction about spiritual powers, together with a very
basic belief that the Christian is precisely the one who is rescued
from the domination of the evil spirits among these powers.

We turn next to the church fathers and then to the great
medieval theologian Thomas Aquinas (who can hardly be called
naive), to look at their beliefs about this realm of being. From
works of philosophy and literature we shall consider a few of the
expressed beliefs about this realm, and in conclusion suggest
very briefly how close the parallel is between the view of the
New Testament and depth psychology's empirical knowledge of
the world of spirit.

The Evidence of the Four Gospels

Jesus' belief in the relationship of human beings to non-
human spiritual reality has not been very popular with Christian
scholars. Indeed, most modern educated Christians have been
brought up to believe that Jesus' concern with the realm of the
angelic and the demonic was determined simply by the world-
view of his time in which he was caught. Thus this aspect of his
ministry must be dismissed as merely the result of a contempo-
rary illusion. At a recent conference of clergymen, when I pro-

posed to discuss the subject of the angelic realm, exactly this objection was raised; and then suddenly the objector said, "Yes, I see. I have simply assumed that my world-view was the correct one and that Jesus' was incorrect—really without ever critically examining them." Yet this is just what we must do, or else naively accept our own assumption about the world, with little basis to question it or see where it leads. To investigate the view of Jesus, we have to start from scratch to explore almost virgin territory.

In the New Testament the three basic words used to describe non-material powers or beings are the Greek words for angel, spirit, and demon. All three can be used to speak of either benevolent or malicious powers. In fact, their primary reference is not to morality but to ontology or being; they refer to entities believed to exist. All of the realities described by these words affect human lives, exercising tremendous influence over men and directing human destiny for good and for ill. In addition we find references to the prince of the demons, to Satan, the evil one, or the devil. Let us take up these words one by one and see just what the New Testament writers meant by them.

Angel

The word *aggelos*, angel, is derived from the Greek word for messenger. It means, in both Old and New Testaments, one of the host of spirits that wait upon some spiritual ruler, some divine monarch. They can be either messengers or instruments and vassals of higher spiritual reality. Thus there are angels of God and angels of Satan; but unless qualified, an angel refers to a good spiritual messenger, a representative of God. In the passage explaining the parable of the sower (Mt. 13:39), angels are seen both as reapers who gather the children of God, and as sent by the Son of Man to take evildoers away to perdition. In Matthew 16:27 we find that the Son of Man will be accompanied by his angels when he comes in the glory of the Father and brings each man his reward.

This idea of the angels of God is expressed over and over again, as in Mark 13:27 and Luke 9:26 and also in the Old Testament. But in Matthew 25:41 Jesus speaks of the devil and his angels and the eternal fire prepared for them, and Revelation 12:7 tells how all hell broke loose on earth when there was war in heaven and the dragon and his angels fought but were cast down to earth. In addition there are the appearances or visions of angels; in all, the missions and appearances of angels are referred to seventy-four times in the gospels and Acts.[4]

In case one objects that angels are never mentioned today, I would like to call attention to a letter which was brought to me about the time I began putting some thoughts together on this subject. It was written by the wife of a clergyman in Jamaica to her daughter, a woman writing about the death of her husband. In it she told how the dying man was sustained by the experience of a heavenly visitation that took away the fear of death and relieved his suffering. It supported his widow and still brings comfort to the daughter. Parts of this letter are reproduced in the footnotes.[5] Similar stories have been told me by a widow and another daughter because they realized I would not make fun of them. The former had not shared the story with anyone else in thirty years of widowhood. Similar stories are reported by Dr. Raymond Moody in *Life After Life* and by Karlis Osis in *Deathbed Observations by Physicians and Nurses.*

Spirit

The second word, *pneuma* or spirit, in some ways seems more intimately connected with human beings than angels, which always seem to come to them from outside themselves. *Pneuma* originally signified a movement of air, which would refer to either the wind or to the breath of man. In Greek literature it had come to mean the vital principle by which the body is animated, and we also find it used to speak of such vital spirit apart from the body. In the first of these senses, spirit is used generally in the gospels to refer to the spirit of Jesus, or in phrases spoken by him as in Matthew 26:41 about the willingness of the spirit. But John speaks about the coming true worship of the Father in spirit and in truth (4:23), and in Acts the spirits of Paul and Stephen are spoken of in much the same way as the spirit of Jesus in the gospels.

In all the other cases, spirits are disembodied; they are independent, non-physical beings on somewhat the same level as human beings, apparently of a lower order than angels or demons. They are capable of knowing, desiring, and acting. In this they can be subject either to God or to Satan, or to other spiritual realities, or even to men and women. These spirits must be clearly distinguished from the Spirit of God, the spiritual reality which partakes of the very nature of God; for one signifies the essence of the Godhead as the other refers to a reality comparable to the spirit or essence of a human being.

Most of the spirits mentioned are malicious and destructive. However, in Paul's letter to the Corinthians he acknowledges the discerning of spirits, or the ability to distinguish between them, thus implying that some must be good (1 Cor. 12:10). In the same letter (14:32) he also speaks of the spirits of the prophets being subject to the prophets. John writes in his first epistle (4:1, New English Bible), "But do not trust any and every spirit, my friends; test the spirits, to see whether they are from God. . . ." In Peter's first letter (3:19) the unfortunate dead are referred to as the spirits in prison. There is also ancient authority for the words of Jesus in Luke 9:55 rebuking an impulse of the disciples by saying, "You do not know what manner of spirit you are of. . . ."

Malicious spirits are described as demonic, unclean, evil, and causing infirmity. In Luke 4:33 there is the demonic spirit which speaks out of the man in the synagogue; Matthew 8:16 and Luke 10:20 also refer to such spirits. There are numerous references to unclean spirits (*pneuma to akatharton*), twenty-one in all in the synoptic gospels and Acts.[6] Other descriptions of these malicious realities are found in the story of the woman bound by a spirit of infirmity (*pneuma asthenias*) in Luke 13:11, and in Mark's story of the boy the disciples could not heal of a dumb spirit (*pneuma alalon*—9:17). There are also several references to evil spirits (*pneuma poneron*), as in Luke 7:21 and 8:2.[7]

Demon

The Greek has two nouns, *daimon* and *daimonion*, for demon, and the verb *daimonizomai*, meaning to be possessed by a demon or demons. In classical Greek the demon was a divine power, a deity or divinity, but the word later took on the lesser meaning of a spirit, either good or bad, a being inferior to God but superior to human beings. While there are one or two references in the New Testament to a *daimon* with whom one might be safely infatuated, as it seems the Greeks often were, all the other allusions to demons describe malignant entities.[8] People possessed by demons, according to Thayer's *Lexicon*, are those suffering from

> . . . especially severe diseases, either bodily or mental (such as paralysis, blindness, deafness, loss of speech, epilepsy, melancholy, insanity, etc.), whose bodies in the opinion of the Jews demons . . . had entered, and so held possession of them as not only to afflict them with ills, but also to dethrone the reason and take its place themselves; accordingly the possessed were wont to express the mind and consciousness of the demons dwelling in them; and their cure was thought to require the expulsion of the demon. . . .[9]

The verb form, describing the state of possession by demons, is found thirteen times in the gospels;[10] and the two nouns, referring to the demonic beings themselves, are spoken of forty-nine times.[11]

Jesus often refers to the prince of the demons as *Satan* or *diabolos*, the devil. *Satan* is the translation of the Hebrew word for adversary; *diabolos* translates the meaning of the Hebrew word for the accuser, the slanderer. He is, according to Thayer, ". . . the prince of demons, the author of evil, persecuting good men . . . estranging mankind from God and enticing them to sin, and afflicting them with diseases by means of demons who take possession of their bodies at his bidding. . . ."[12] He is known by several other names quite descriptive of his reality. In the Lord's prayer Jesus asks that we be delivered from the Evil One. He is the prince of this world (Jn. 12:31), the prince of darkness (Eph. 6:12), a roaring lion and an adversary (1 Pet. 5:8), Beelzebub (Mt. 12:24). In Revelation he shows up as the serpent (20:2), the dragon (12:7), and the angel of the bottomless pit (9:11). To Paul in 2 Corinthians, he is the god of this world (4:4). Obviously demonic powers were seen as working in organization, with Satan, the Evil One, or the devil at their head, and he is called by one name or another in fifty places in the gospels and Acts.[13] There can be little doubt that the concept of subsidiary and evil spiritual beings was an integral part of the thought of Jesus and the authors of the New Testament.

The Psychology of Jesus

In order to realize the importance of Jesus' ideas about demon possession, it is necessary to see how they influence his theory of personality, and how that theory of personality influenced his whole approach to human beings. One might even say that the ethics of Jesus do not make sense except as we see human beings between two worlds, with the world of the demonic impinging upon them and sometimes possessing individuals against their will. To get a clear picture of Jesus' actual point of view about the nature of human personality, we must first of all be able to sketch our own and see how different it is from the point of view of Jesus. We can then see which is more realistic and workable.

One Current Theory of Personality

There is a commonly accepted, implied theory of personality current in our Western world, although most of the people who hold it have never stated it clearly or even awakened to the fact that they hold to such a psychology of personality. This naive, tacit theory runs something like this: Personality is relatively simple, relatively easy to understand; it is only a matter of conditioned reflexes. Basically, all humans have complete control of themselves and their actions. They determine what they do by their own conscious choices. *Therefore*, if they have knowledge of what is right and wrong, expedient or inappropriate, they will do the good or expedient if their wills are good, and the evil or foolishly inexpedient if their wills are bad. *Therefore* (and this *therefore* is even larger than the first), if a human being does anything that is silly or evil or illegal with knowledge that the act is silly or evil or illegal, it is because that person *wanted to do the silly or evil or illegal thing.*

Thus, according to this point of view, evil action is the result of bad will; and bad will can be changed only by punishment. If you punish human beings enough, they will change; and if they do not respond, then it is because their will is bad, irredeemably bad. Thus, the normally sane human being is a single-minded, integrated personality, knowing what he/she is doing and why, and capable of controlling himself/herself at all times if he/she really wishes to. The task of society and of the parent is simply to educate and to punish. Incredible as it may seem, most people's view of themselves—the implicit, popular view—follows this outline with hardly a bulge. So long as a person is not psychotic to the point of being unable to perceive reality, that person is entirely responsible for his/her actions. No wonder that love is so rare a commodity in our society. It has little place in the unconscious psychology of today.

That which is never brought out into the open and stated can never be criticized. This view, which lies at the base of most of our theories about human beings, is accepted with so little question that it is seldom even glanced at. Though it forms the very basis of our relations with other people, it is seldom challenged by the person in the street or even by the clergy. Unless we have run into serious personal problems, been faced with serious mental illness among those with whom we live closely, have seriously studied the problem of emotional difficulties (and made clinical observations as part of that study), or have fallen deeply in love, few of us ever question this general view of human personality. And the tragedy is that this naive theory of personality, which goes into forming our world-view, is woefully inadequate.

It is on this theory about people that *modern* legal theories are based. Thus, if it can be shown that people were capable of knowing what they were doing when they broke the law, they receive the full force of the law's retribution. Because the law is based upon an antiquated point of view, people who are obviously emotionally incapable of controlling their actions by all modern medical standards are sent to prison and to death by the courts. It is upon the basis of the same theory that ineffective penal institutions are run which return most of the criminals back to society more convinced than ever of continuing in crime. It is upon the same basis of the same theory of psychology that most mental institutions have been run until recently, and some still continue, doing little but imprison their patients. It is on the basis of this theory that most neighborhood quarrels and hurt feelings and gossip get started. It is upon this thinking of this theory that children are emotionally starved and battered. Human personality has not been changed very often by the practices based on this theory. A bad will is not changed; it is simply put out of society's way.

Jesus' Theory

Jesus' theory of human personality was quite different. He treated human beings as far more complex. He did not ignore conscious control; on the contrary, he believed and taught that, up to a point, people do have conscious control of personality and should exercise and develop it. So much, in fact, did Jesus stress the importance of this control of the instinctual life that it became one of the marks of Christian society and has expanded more in those societies influenced by the teachings of Jesus than anywhere else in the world. Indeed, we have seen conscious control grow to the point of becoming a positive inducement to neurosis.

On the other hand, Jesus believed that humans could also be influenced by *spiritual powers*—by non-material, psychic reality. He repeatedly referred to the angels of God or to the Son of Man and his angels. He himself was driven by the Spirit into the wilderness and there had to confront the devil. Humans could be helped, directed or enlightened by positive spiritual powers. But Jesus also believed that they could be possessed by alien powers, unclean spirits, evil spirits, demons, satanic forces, and that this could happen against their wills and even unknown to them. Demonic spirits made people sick physically, mentally, and morally. The conscious will was set aside by the alien power, and once this had happened a man's will was in no position to control a demon. The person's power of knowing was not necessarily impaired at all; he could know very well that he was possessed and still be able to do nothing about it. It was a matter of will, of being unable to act at all, not of knowledge.

It is very interesting how modern Christian theology has passed over these statements and stories about demon possession in the New Testament as if they were afraid to look at the facts for fear of making Jesus look silly. How little confidence such Christianity has in Jesus of Nazareth. These demonic forces form such a basic part of the gospel tradition that to ignore the stories, actions and beliefs about them is to leave untouched a whole segment of Jesus' life and practice—just because we find this part difficult to harmonize with our particular world-view and its implicit psychological belief. These passages form such an integral part of Jesus' thought and teaching and practice, however, that it is simply impossible for us, ignoring them, to comprehend his concept of human nature. If we reject these passages as silly, we come very close to rejecting Jesus as silly.

He also spoke of achieving the single eye, implying that human beings could be other than single-eyed, single-minded, that there might be more than one center of personality and will within an individual, and that one of them could well be demonic or divine. He also spoke again and again (it is almost the keynote of the gospel) of losing one's life to find it. Whatever else this means, it certainly implies that there are various levels of personality and that to gain one of them another has to be sacrificed.

The importance of these concepts can hardly be overestimated for understanding Jesus and the New Testament and the necessity of discernment. One has to give up one's own will so that God's will (in other words, God's spirit or the Holy Spirit) can become the center of one's life and personality. The human will or ego cannot stand against demonic infiltration and possession unless one is endowed by the Spirit of God which protects a person. Our humanity alone is not enough to deal with the depth and complexity of psychic life in which each individual participates; pure humanity alone is not able to stand against the demonic. One reason that Jesus is so hostile to sickness and sin is that they result from domination of the human being by an alien spirit. Jesus' whole being was hostile to this negative reality. Dr. C. G. Jung, the Swiss psychiatrist, stated more than once that most of human evil comes from the unconscious. Whatever else

we say about human beings, we must confess that the unconscious possesses most of them; that it is often just another way of
saying that evil possesses them. They are not in full conscious
control of themselves and so fall into destructiveness.

Consequences of Jesus' Theory

What are the practical consequences of this point of view
about human beings? In the first place, people are not totally
responsible for all their evil or their sickness. They are possessed, and so they deserve our understanding, indeed our compassion in its root meaning. Everyone is bearing a heavier burden
than we realize, for all men and women are struggling, whether
they know it or not, against powers of spiritual darkness. Thus,
our reaction toward our fellow men will be governed by compassion rather than moralism. Indeed, this very compassion is what
most people are searching for to carry them through their dismal
struggle.

In the second place, people who are possessed cannot
change simply by an exercise of will, but only as a power greater
than themselves is brought to bear upon them. Thus our love
and understanding may give them the necessary power to unseat
what is governing them, while knowledge and moralistic advice
do not work to unseat it. Moralism is seldom enough. In most
cases punishment weakens the conscious will and gives the destructive forces yet more reign in our lives. As for knowledge,
most people already know full well what is the matter with them
but lack the power to change. When humans are really battered
and bruised, only a power coming to them from the outside
really helps them. Most of us need good pastoring and tender,
loving care.

In the third place (and this is a corollary of the second
point), religion which brings the individual into contact with the
positive and creative forces in the universe is the only way to
effect a lasting and vital moral transformation in a person. Any
other kind of religion results in an attempt to encase the individual, to possess him with a one-sided, split-off idea of life, and
often is a good bit worse than useless. Only as the spirit of God,

the Holy Spirit, with what may be called the hosts of heaven, comes to human aid, can they become what they wish to become and fight off the assault of the demonic which surrounds them. Change takes place most often through contact with a loving God.

Apostolic and Patristic Ideas

One of the basic apostolic ideas about Christ and the church was that as individuals participated in the church, and in the spirit of Christ or the Holy Spirit, they were given deliverance from the forces of evil under which they had been in subjection. The apostles called these forces of evil—which result in moral, mental and physical illness—by a variety of colorful names. Whether they were called demons, angels, principalities, powers, the flesh, the law, sin, death, thrones, dominions, authorities or beggarly elements, human beings were known to be under their dominion, and one of the important reasons for the coming of Christ, for his death and resurrection, was to rescue people from them. Somehow in his submission to these powers in death, and in his victory over them in his resurrection, he has gained the power to share the same victory with men and women who partake of his spirit.

To Paul and the other New Testament writers, as well as to Jesus, the world of these spiritual entities was very real indeed. Men and women were beset by beings from a spiritual realm which has elements of both good and evil in it. If human beings were to escape being overcome by the evil elements, the forces abroad in the world which seek their destruction, they must take real religion seriously, enlisting the help of the Holy Spirit, the church, and positive spiritual forces. Salvation then was not just a matter of moral perfectionism. Salvation was the result of a battle in which we were rescued from the evil in the world, and that evil is a very real one; it is evil in the form of malignant spiritual entities which afflict us in many subtle ways. About this Paul is very clear. He writes in Galatians:

Formerly, when you did not know God, you were in bondage to beings that by nature are no gods; but now that you have come to know God, or rather to be known by God, how can you turn back again to the weak and beggarly elemental spirits, whose slaves you want to be once more? (4:8-9).

He concludes his magnificent thanksgiving for salvation in Romans by saying that none of these evil powers can touch the one who has known the love of God in Christ Jesus:

For I am sure that neither death, nor life, nor angels, nor principalities, nor things present, nor things to come, nor powers, nor height, nor depth, nor anything else in all creation, will be able to separate us from the love of God in Christ Jesus our Lord (8:38-39).

This is not just nice poetry; it is spiritual realism. In Colossians Paul states that Christ "disarmed the principalities and powers and made a public example of them, triumphing over them" in the cross and resurrection (2:15).

Whether Ephesians is by Paul's hand or not makes little difference. It speaks the same basic attitude toward the spiritual realm that surrounds us:

Finally, be strong in the Lord and in the strength of his might. Put on the whole armor of God, that you may be able to stand against the wiles of the devil. For we are not contending against flesh and blood, but against the principalities, against the powers, against the world rulers of this present darkness, against the spiritual hosts of wickedness in the heavenly places (6:10-12).

Essentially the same idea is found in the first epistle of Peter:

Baptism, which corresponds to this, now saves you, not as a removal of dirt from the body but as an appeal to God for a clear conscience, through the resurrection of Jesus Christ, who has gone into heaven and is at the right hand of God, with angels, authorities, and powers subject to him (3:21-22).

The writings of apostolic times abound with angels, especially in their benevolent role. They appear twenty-one times in Acts; there are thirty references throughout the epistles; and, of course, Revelation is simply brimming over with them. Twice Paul calls attention to bad angels, in 2 Corinthians 11:14 and Colossians 2:18. The devil is acknowledged again and again, in forty passages in these books, often in accordance with the belief of the time that he was but one of the fallen spiritual beings. Evil spirits crop up and are dealt with at least eight times in Acts, and there are a few scattered references to demons in subsequent books.

This last emphasis is a major difference from the gospels. It is one in which the apostolic writers are appealing for a real depth of understanding, which was never fully given in later centuries. Paul, and probably the other authors of the epistles, had to keep in mind that they were addressing churches in communities that were anything but monotheistic. The Greeks were thoroughly familiar with demons, both the good ones and the spiteful, and we might say that when they did not respect and worship the power of the gods and such beings, they were at least enamored with it. Spiritual beings were a part of the Graeco-Roman culture. Furthermore, Paul certainly had had some experience himself with the power of the devil and what it meant to be released from it. Hence the language of passages like those we have quoted lumps the familiar spiritual entities into descriptions that are calculated to make the tyrannical and despotic side of their nature pretty clear.

There is no question but that the same spiritual beings are referred to as the demons and evil spirits of the gospels, and they are found in Acts, Romans, 1 and 2 Corinthians, Galatians, Ephesians, Colossians, 1 and 2 Thessalonians, 1 and 2 Timothy, Hebrews 1 and 2 Peter, 1 and 2 John, Jude and Revelation. This is very nearly a catalogue of the New Testament letters.[14]

Early Church Writers

This emphasis upon the spiritual realm continued in the early writing of the church, where we find the same concern with spiritual realities other than man or God himself. Indeed one could say that references to these beings were nearly as frequent in the pages of the ante-Nicene fathers as in the pages of the New Testament. This was the climate in which these men thought and moved. They believed in a spiritual world of spiritual entities which had important consequences for human lives, and they also believed that some of these beings were malignant and some good.

Origen taught that angels do exist, citing the fact that the church had always had this belief, although he did not believe that he could explain what they are or why they exist. He also believed that the devil was an angel who became apostate and induced many angels to fall away with him. But because some of these angels have fallen away does not change their basic nature as servants in accomplishing the salvation of human beings. At one point Origen referred to Hebrews 1:14 to support this idea, and he wrote many pages discussing the various angels and their heavenly tasks. The angels are ministering spirits, not gods or some other race of being. Their purpose is to bear the supplications of people to heavenly places in the universe, and then return to people, conferring on them the benefits of God. Angels devote themselves to God and they dispose of the hostility of demons. They know who is worthy of divine approval and they cooperate with these people in their endeavor to please God. There are similar discussions in Clement of Rome and also in the Shepherd of Hermas, the Epistle of Barnabas, and two works of Ignatius.[15]

Justin Martyr, Methodius, and Lactantius all discuss the transgressions of the angels and their fall at some length and in a way not nearly so metaphysical as the ideas of Revelation. Originally, they tell, God committed the care of humans and all things under heaven to angels. But the angels transgressed their trust by falling in love with women and begetting children who turned out to be demons. Thus fallen and reinforced, they subdue the human race through magical writings, fears and punishments, teaching humans to offer sacrifices, sowing murders, wars, adulteries, and all wickedness. Instead of protecting people, they are now busy bedeviling the very creatures they were sent to care for.[16]

Augustine was deeply concerned with the reality of angelic and demonic powers and kept them constantly before the reader of his *Confessions*, *City of God*, and other works. They form an essential part of his thinking about salvation. He asks, after all, what is man or woman to be saved from? It is the demonic world, and one of the great agencies committed to this work is the very positive host of heaven.[17]

In his scholarly study of the atonement, *Christus Victor*, Gustaf Aulén has shown how consistently this point of view was held by the early church. His essential thesis is that, for these people, atonement is the conviction that Christ in his crucifixion and resurrection overcame the demonic entities that afflict humans, and thus ransomed and freed humans from them.[18] This was the commonly held belief until the time of Anselm, and it has remained essential to the thinking of Greek Orthodoxy throughout the centuries.

Thomas Aquinas

The medieval theologian, Thomas Aquinas, was known as the angelic doctor not because of his shining virtue but because of his great concern for these beings and his belief in their power and influence over the lives of people. Although for the past two centuries those pages in Aquinas which treat of angels have been looked upon with scorn by non-Catholics and with some embarrassment by Catholics themselves who have read them, the truths they contain still stand. We have not done away with angels by treating them with holy neglect. Father White in *God and the Unconscious*, from which I have already quoted, devotes three chapters to demonstrating quite clearly the reality of the angelic and demonic.[19] There is nothing naive or childish about Aquinas' discussion of angels. Rather they form an essential part of Thomistic thought.

To Aquinas, good angels are the carriers of revelation to people, while the evil ones are the source of most of people's problems and difficulties. It is a purely mental and not a physical reality to which he refers as an angel. This is no proverbial discussion of how many angels can stand on the head of a pin; Aquinas is dealing with a different reality. He calls them *intelligibilia intelligentia*, or "thinking thoughts." Like our own conscious thinking and thoughts, they were effective in bringing about changes in events in the corporeal world. But this is as far as he goes in discussing how an angel acts upon the soul or psyche.

Father White fills in, giving first Jung's definition of unconscious complexes as "groups of psychic contents, isolated from consciousness, functioning arbitrarily and autonomously, leading thus a life of their own in the unconscious; whence they can at any moment hinder or further conscious acts."[20] Then he goes on:

> The definition might be a very good description of Thomist devils—or angels. . . . Our contention is that the meanings of the two sets of terms (the theological and the psychopathological) are, however, not mutually exclusive; and we would offer for expert consideration the suggestion that, while the meanings are different, each term may be, and commonly is, referable to the selfsame phenomenon or occurrence.[21]

The real difficulty, which Aquinas did not overcome, was that he was tied to the philosophy of Aristotle, and so he had to make the experience of angels far more complicated outwardly than necessary, and so also their influence upon human beings. He believed that only as these spiritual beings influenced outside matter, which then had an effect upon us, or as they influenced our bodies so as to stir up our imagination (particularly through the liver and the bile), and only thus, did we have any contact with this realm of being. Aquinas was so determined to preserve people's free will that he could not believe that these heavenly creatures could have any direct contact or influence upon our psyches or upon our wills. Yet it would seem that they do; and this also appears to be what Jesus thought. When a person is possessed by an autonomous complex, he is directly possessed by something other than himself, and not through any roundabout agency, either. I doubt if we are as free as Aquinas wanted to believe. Freedom is more a matter of degree than black and white.

St. Thomas' discussion of how the angels fell, of what went wrong, is a long one. According to his view, the prince of angels fell because of his pride, his desire to be God in place of God; and it was this that led to the rift between heaven and hell. From this came people's problem of being beset with evil, and so the necessity for the protection of the church and the Holy Spirit. If one is tempted to smile and murmur, "Surely this was the last serious tome about angels," we must remember that leaders of both the Renaissance and the Reformation continued this concern. Among them were Luther, Calvin and Schleiermacher, who went right on with the investigation of non-human spiritual beings. And we need to remember that Aquinas' thinking was normative in the Catholic Church until Vatican II.

Philosophical and Literary Spirits

It is also interesting to note that angels were considered a respectable subject of discussion among the most elevated philosophical groups up until about two hundred years ago. The ancient philosophers spoke of the inferior gods and of the nature spirits, and discussed the matter of intelligences other than human in the universe. It may be hard to realize that secular philosophers through the centuries, who were far more interested in science and politics than in religion, continued to give serious consideration to non-physical beings, but it is true. Hobbes, for instance, wrote, "As in the resurrection men shall be permanent and not incorporeal, so therefore also are the angels." Locke also discussed the subject of spiritual bodies and angels at some length, holding that we "are able to frame the complex idea of an immaterial spirit." Bacon, in *Novum Organum*, likewise discussed the difference between the human and the angelic mind. Leibniz and Pascal also thought and wrote on the same subject.[22]

If we turn to the great literary productions, we find again the same concern with non-physical beings. Remember the appearances of ghosts and witches and other kinds of spirits in Shakespeare's plays? If all the allusions to such things were removed from his works, we would emasculate some of his most important plays. The ghost in Hamlet, for one, has recently been the subject of a most productive psychological study.[23] Dante, again, took many pages of his *Divine Comedy* to consider the subject of angels; Goethe's *Faust* and Chaucer's *Canterbury Tales*, both built thematically around elements as down to earth as those in Faulkner or Dreiser, are also swarming with denizens of the non-physical world. One of the greatest works of English literature, Milton's *Paradise Lost*, was written for the direct purpose of dealing with the fall of Satan and his angels and the horrible consequences for humans. The works of Blake and Poe also treat of this realm in great depth.

The last hundred and fifty years have not seen the death of interest within the literary world in the spiritual realm and the devil, but what might be called the "return of the devil." Early in this period James Hogg wrote a book, *The Private Memoirs and Confessions of a Justified Sinner*, which has been called by some the English *Faust*.

In the same period Percy Bysshe Shelley's wife wrote *Frankenstein*, the story which was based on a dream and which has been a horror thriller ever since. Robert Louis Stevenson's first success, fifty years later, was also a mythological story based on a dream; *Dr. Jekyll and Mr. Hyde* caught the imagination of the English people who had intellectually rejected the idea of evil. The story expressed the dualism of Victorian England as nothing else could. Another example of what the literary mind coughed up in that enlightened age was Bram Stoker's *Dracula* which has fascinated people ever since and given thrills of horror to modern people who thought that life was dull.

Although the church had buried the devil along with secular society's concern for evil, he was soon showing up again in George MacDonald's *Phantastes* and *Lilith*, and those novels inspired C. S. Lewis. His magnificent fantasy novels tell the story of evil first in cosmic terms—he started with a trip to another planet—and then in a series of children's stories. In *The Screwtape Letters* he also catches the devil himself in a *camera obscura*. Charles Williams, an Anglican clergyman, was even more concerned that the church consider the reality of spiritual evil and take it very seriously. His study on *Witchcraft* traces historically the devotion to spiritual evil, and in seven amazingly constructed novels he makes the point over and over again that just because something is spiritual does not mean it is good. Evil is just as real as good and those who do not deal with it, and suffer consciously in their struggle against it, are overcome and destroyed by it. One finds the same point of view in the mythological masterpieces of Tolkien, *The Hobbit* and *The Lord of the Rings*, and also in T. S. Eliot's work, particularly in *Murder in the Cathedral* and *The Cocktail Party*.

The novels of Hermann Hesse have made a real splash within the college community in recent years. These novels express many of the ideas of Jung, and the characters move in and out of a non-physical world. At the time that I write these words the four books of Carlos Castaneda and the tales of Indian shamanism are the most popular books on American college campuses. This reflects the interest of young people in the reality of the spiritual world. And then there is *The Exorcist* which made a mint first as a novel and then in its film version. The interest in evil is not dead.

It is, however, the detective story which expresses the current interest in evil better than anything else. The "who-done-it" presents evil in the form of murder, then the question of discernment in discovering the culprit, and then the final bringing of the criminal to justice. Dr. McGlashan has called attention to the fact that the comics with their cartoons almost always represent archetypal figures; also the detective story gives mythological form to the problem of evil today.

The Problem of Evil as a Reality

The reality of evil which the Second World War produced brought certain thinkers to a consideration of the Christian religion and its essential meaning. In England Cyril Joad, a former agnostic philosopher, has expressed a profound philosophy in *The Recovery of Belief*, maintaining that the rationalistic rejection of evil is no longer satisfactory, since it does not account for the facts of experience. Jung, in reaching the same conclusion, has written that the concentration camps of Nazi Germany can hardly be described as an accidental absence of perfection. Yet most religion and nearly all science stubbornly refuse to see the reality of evil which mythology proclaims. The former results in experts-on-the-soul who cannot handle prejudice or neurosis, while the latter perpetrates the "boy Fausts" on the world, as Gerald Sykes has called nuclear physicists who disclaim their share in producing atomic devastation. Neither group can deal with what it does not face.

Jung began to study the problem of evil when he realized that a person cannot fight to overcome evil until he/she believes in its reality. He found that most of his patients could be released from neurotic fear and childish giving in to evil only by taking it very seriously. He also found that mythology and its images and symbols were indispensable in this undertaking. *Rationality alone cannot deal with evil.* Evil is not rational in nature, and until a person recaptures his/her mythological sense, he/she has difficulty getting onto the field where battle is done with evil. It overcomes the person first, or else he/she is unconsciously dominated by it. Many people have called Jung a Gnostic or Manichean because of his emphasis on the reality of evil. Nothing could be further from the truth. If one will allow oneself to experience something of what Jung describes in the chapter of his autobiography on the "Confrontation with the Unconscious," one will realize that Jung deals with experiences, not just ideas about experiences. He simply says that evil cannot be intellectually dismissed or removed. It can only be struggled with, for evil is an existential fact. The devil is empirically true, and it can no more be removed by looking away than the chair in which I sit.

Depth Psychology and the Spiritual Realm

In the work of Carl Jung we find that this realm of being can be treated empirically and with respect by a scientifically-minded person of today, and that he/she does not just wipe it off the blackboard with scientific understanding. I, for one, am sometimes abashed to think that it has taken a doctor of medicine, rather than one of theology, to convince even a few people that the New Testament is to be taken seriously, not scaled and cleaned like a fish.

The Collective Unconscious

Dr. Jung has met and described a vast realm of being, both in himself and his patients, which he calls the objective psyche, or the collective unconscious. It is given by direct contact with the human psyche and is similar to the human psyche, and thus it is the very part of all creation we are most likely to treat with contempt, feeling all too familiar with it. But, as Jung has shown, a person's consciousness of individual relationship to the collective unconscious which becomes individual being has developed last of all, and this consciousness presents him/her with the most mysterious and inexhaustible realm he/she approaches. Jung has written:

> . . . the spontaneous utterances of the unconscious do after all reveal a psyche which is not identical with consciousness and which is, at times, greatly at variance with it. These utterances occur as a natural psychic activity that can neither be learnt nor controlled by the will. The manifestation of the unconscious is therefore a revelation of the unknown in man. We have only to disregard the dependence of dream language on environment and substitute "eagle" for "aeroplane," "dragon" for "automobile" or "train," "snake-bite" for "injection," and so forth, in order to arrive at the more universal and more fundamental language of mythology. This gives us access to the primordial images that underlie all thinking and have a considerable influence even on our scientific ideas. In these archetypal forms, something, presumably, is expressing itself that must in some way be connected with the mysterious operation of a natural psyche—in other words, with a cosmic factor of the first order.[24]

Immaterial but Real

Thus Dr. Jung has expressed again and again, in connection with all kinds of experiences, the fact that men and women are in contact with a realm of being which is not material, but which is just as real—no, perhaps more real and important—than the material world. And they are in contact with it whether they like it or not. He has suggested this clearly to questioning minds by the uncanny accuracy with which he can describe a personality from archetypal material found in the person's dreams. In the same book he has said, with a bit of tongue-in-cheek:

Quite apart from merely personal prejudices, the psyche assimilates external facts in its own way   the laws or patterns of apperception . . . do not change, although different ages or different parts of the world call them by different names. On a primitive level people are afraid of witches; on the modern level we are apprehensively aware of microbes. There everybody believes in ghosts, here everybody believes in vitamins. Once upon a time men were possessed by devils, now they are not less obsessed by ideas . . . . [25]

People who do not live partly in this world, who exist only as conscious, purposive egos (and this Dr. Jung also contends) are mere fragments of themselves. Without the meaning and intelligence of this inner world, people are likely to live in one area of life, in a dining room, or a workroom, and blame everyone else for the shadows in corners they are afraid to poke into.

"The tremendous power of the 'objective psychic,' " again according to Jung, "has been named 'demon' or 'God' in all epochs with the sole exception of the recent present. We have become so bashful in matters of religion that we correctly say 'unconscious,' because God has in fact become unconscious to us."[26] And so, we may add, the devil has become unconscious as well. In a study of the psychological factors present in the Nazi catastrophe, Jung wrote in 1945:

Just when people were congratulating themselves on having abolished all spooks, it turned out that instead of haunting the attic or old ruins the spooks were flitting about in the heads of apparently normal Europeans. Tyrannical, obsessive, intoxicating ideas and delusions were abroad everywhere, and people began to believe the most absurd things, just as the possessed do.[27]

In the early years of the 1960's Dr. Jung answered a letter written to him by Bill Wilson, the founder of AA. In it is one of his latest and most explicit references to the reality of evil: "I am strongly convinced that . . . an ordinary man, not protected by an action from above and isolated in society, cannot resist the power of evil, which is called very aptly the Devil. But the use of such words arouses so many mistakes that one can only keep aloof from them. . . ."[28] Those who have seen the destructive effect of alcoholism can certainly see in it the full fury of the powers of evil. Such possession, Jung believed, had more to do with the rise of Nazism than economic or any other factors.

Knowledge of the Spiritual Realm

When people are aware of their relation to spiritual reality, they stand a chance of sitting in on its councils; otherwise, they become merely its pawns. God wants people who know Him, while the devil's best stratagem is simply to convince people that he does not exist. But as everyone who enters this realm discovers, the distinguishable realities, the entities—almost personal-ities—do exist, even when we see them only abstracted as ideas or obsessions. Jung has observed them, and he has described them as complexes and archetypes; the church, as angels and demons. A rose by any other name. . . .[29]

Thus the field of clinical psychology offers direct, observable evidence that what the church for centuries has talked about as angelic forces and powers, as thrones, principalities, dominions, and authorities, as demons and devils, are in fact real. Such words refer to certain non-physical realities which do impinge upon us and influence us all. By rejecting them as the illusion of an archaic time, we moderns are rejecting what men everywhere have thought true *except* those with the attitude and belief of Western Europe and America since the mid-eighteenth century.

As Dr. Jung has suggested, isn't it just possible that the most neurotic and upset peoples the world has seen may well be off on the wrong foot? This part of the world, which has caused more destructive war and chaos in sixty or eighty years than we find in the rest of history, may just be ignorant, having overlooked an important half of life and reality. Real understanding of these realities will not depotentiate the Christian gospel or alter a word of its truth. Rather, an intelligent comprehension of them adds weight to the entire creed we base on the New Testament record.

An interesting story about the reality of the Evil One comes from the committee which was preparing the final revision of the Book of Common Prayer for the Episcopal Church. When this group came to the subject of the baptismal office there was real division about including the words about renouncing Satan and all his works. It was at this time that the film *The Exorcist* was drawing tremendous crowds. Heated discussion followed. Instead of avoiding reference to the Devil the following questions were inserted in the baptismal office:

Question Do you renounce Satan and all the spiritual forces of wickedness that rebel against God?
Answer   I renounce them.
Question Do you renounce the evil powers of this world which corrupt and destroy the creatures of God?
Answer   I renounce them.[30]

Conclusions for Discernment

What conclusions then, can we draw from considering the angelic and the demonic realities?

1. What the New Testament refers to as demons and angels are realities or non-physical entities which need to be taken into consideration if human beings would make the most out of life. Among them are both positive and negative forces, the one leading individuals forward and the other prodding them to destruction. The first step is simply for a person to come into conscious awareness of this realm. That which you know is much more likely to be dealt with adequately than that which you don't know. Even a good boxer would find it harder to meet an opponent who sneaks up to him in the dark than one who faces him in the ring.

2. Human beings need salvation. They need help to guide them through the conflicting forces and powers and entities that surround them. This is not just a polite addition to an already good life. The good life consists in finding the power to withstand evil and be brought to wholeness. If there is no devil and nothing really demonic, then the historic Christian church is a mountain

travailing to bring forth a mouse. But this is far from the experience of most people. There *is* something to be saved from, and if a person is not saved, then there is destruction, often the kind hidden behind a scrapbook of success or an elegant mansion or well-bred children, and which comes out only after the third cocktail. There are non-material realities conniving against one to bring one low. One needs to develop discernment to recognize them and be guided toward salvation.

3. Salvation is not an easy thing to achieve, or God would not have gone to such trouble to buy it for us by the death and resurrection of his Son. This is something we can hardly do for ourselves or by ourselves. We need the spirit and power of God, the Holy Spirit. Human beings can be saved only by a vital religion that brings them into contact with the living spirit of the living God. Only this spirit can guide them through the difficulties of life toward God and wholeness. It is no easy matter to discern which is the way of the Spirit.

4. The person who plays with the demonic or toys with it may come to real tragedy. These forces must be put aside, renounced. Human beings who think they are strong enough to make their own deal with these forces are in danger.

5. The myth of the fall of Satan does not exactly belong in a storybook for children. It is one of our most valuable ways of realizing the evil in the world and how we should deal with it. It says that those of us who try to run our own lives by ourselves are in danger; after all, Satan's only fault was that he thought he could run heaven better than God. And how often do we act this way about our own lives? We need to discern how much of our activity is dominated by egocentricity and pride, the qualities of Lucifer.

6. We must let it sink in that we live in a much more mysterious and wonderful world than we ordinarily realize—a world of depths and heights, of numinous power, of incredible good and evil, of spooky and inexhaustible beings. In short, we find a world well worth some trouble, even the trouble of seeking the salvation

it can offer. How much we need the gift of discernment to see these things as they are and distinguish the good from the evil.

7. On the other hand, some people can become overawed by this spiritual world and fail to see that they have any control. It is easy for human beings to shirk responsibility and blame their problems on others. Demonic forces can be used in the same way. They can say in that situation: "The devil made me do it." Such people forget that, once they have recognized that the demonic is at hand, *they have the responsibility to see that it does not take over in their lives.* People with no control over what is done through them are sick individuals. They need help. They need help to develop and become. If they do not recognize the need of help they may have to be restrained in order not to do damage to themselves and others.

"The Devil made me do it" is pure cop-out when used as an excuse for a repeated problem. One purpose of consciousness and will is to give us the weight with which to tip the scales away from the demonic and toward the divine. Sometimes one cannot handle a problem directly. It is necessary to have divine help. For example, Robert Thomsen's biography, *Bill W.*, shows clearly the many factors involved in alcoholism. The alcoholic is simply unable to control drinking by will power alone.

8. Human beings are deeper and more complex than we ordinarily realize. Many things that appear demonic within us are actually rejected parts of ourselves. They have broken unceremoniously into our lives because we have refused to look at all of us and so have failed to work at integration and wholeness. The evil in this situation is not that which has broken out like a starving wolf; it is more like a dog breaking loose because we have tied it up and forgotten to feed it. We have refused to see our animal naturalness and take care of it. We shall say more about this later.

There is likewise a danger in seeing everything which resists our narrow ego point of view as demonic. There is a veritable craze in some circles to exorcise, to cast out the demonic through ritual means. Without real discernment this can be *very* dangerous. If one tries to exorcise the natural parts of a human being which have reared their heads because they have been ignored, exorcism can lead to a one-sided, impoverished and truncated personality.

Likewise if the problem is one of ego strength, of the capacity and ability to distinguish between the inner and outer worlds and to deal with both of them, exorcism is not only not effective but *dangerous*. People with this kind of weakness need the best psychiatric help and often confinement in a hospital to keep them from hurting themselves and others. Psychosis and neurosis are seldom healed by exorcism. It is not a matter of casting something out, but of building the individual up to resist evil. The inability to contain evil may be due to lack of development of personality and ego-strength rather than to possession.

John Richards in the closing pages of his book *But Deliver Us from Evil* tells a story of a teenage youth who came into a church with a knife. He was disarmed and went his way but a few days later murdered a young boy. The Rev. Mr. Richards seemed to think that exorcism could have solved the problem. I rather believe that the situation is a clear example of one needing psychiatric attention. I doubt very much if exorcism would have been a permanent solution to this person's problem.

Discernment in this instance requires a knowledge not only of the spiritual realm, but of the psychological as well. It is always better to be safe than sorry. In most instances where there has been an intrusion of the demonic, where autonomous complexes have taken over a life, pastoral care is far more effective and long-lasting than exorcism. In real pastoral care and good counseling the individual personality is strengthened so that it can resist the evil and will throw its weight toward balancing the scales by opening the door to the powers of light.

9. Let us see if we can be more specific about the characteristics of demonic influences as opposed to angelic and divine influences. How can we tell from the outside which kind of influence is operating in an individual or a group?

a. The first question to ask in this regard is whether the action or statement of belief of an individual or group is in accord with some tradition, some coherent body of religious beliefs. When a course of action departs from a traditional one and in no way tries to relate to any tradition, this is a danger signal that something other than the divine may be operating.

On the other hand when the individual or group is rigidly bound to the letter of the law of some religious group and can conceive of nothing new, then the spirit of death rather than life is often at work. Sometimes religious groups are used to provide security for insecure people. Sometimes by excessive authoritarianism they actually foster immaturity, and this is not of God. Those who are touched by the Holy Spirit are no longer so immature. They know the reality of God's love, and they respect the traditional way, yet they know that in any human institution there is room for growth. The angelic promotes this kind of spirit.

b. The second question to ask is whether the action which we are discerning results in love and harmony or in hate and schism. The angelic nearly always facilitates and results in love and improved inter-relationships. Those who claim to have angelic inspiration and preach hate and division need to be watched very carefully. Seldom, very seldom, does the angelic result in division. Few issues are large enough to justify separation of brothers and sisters. Likewise the truly angelic seldom speaks in judgment of others. Few people are converted by judgment. The angelic never gloats over a destructive or judgmental message.

c. Jesus spoke with authority and not with finality. Those who claim angelic inspiration and claim to know the specifics of final truth before which all others must bow may well be deceived. Evil and the demonic are far less open to growth and development than the angelic. Jesus said we do not know the time or the hour. Those who claim such knowledge are claiming to know more than he. Some demagogues speak with complete certainty in order to give security to frightened people. This can be a way of gaining power over others, and this is not the way of the angelic.

d. If an action or way of life has angelic inspiration and guidance, it will result in the fruits of creativity, growth, development, increased consciousness and keener awareness. The demonic usually results in disintegration, narrowed awareness and stunted growth. Neurotic stagnation is often the result of demonic influence.

e. One nearly sure sign of demonic power is the attempt on the part of one person or group to gain power over others and seek from the others an attitude of subservence. The angelic stimulates freedom and open and honest exchange between people. The demonic favors bondage and class distinction. Whenever one person seeks to gain power over another, one can almost be sure that the angelic is not at work.

The angelic seeks to promote the attitude of love, encounter and interchange. It rejects dependency on any long-range basis and seeks to create conditions which will enable all people to stand on their own feet and have their own relationship with God and an equal relationship with other human beings.

f. The demonic uses; the angelic encounters. Seldom are people possessed by the angelic. Whenever people use others for their own gain or desires, one can be sure that they are under demonic influence. For this reason slavery is one of the worst of human evils. God and the angelic want to relate to us as free beings, not to own us. The demonic wishes to possess us and drag us down into the kingdom of hell. Whenever a person seeks to own or possess or use another, beware. The Evil One is close.

g. When one gets inflated and thinks of oneself as perfect and then projects one's shadow and darkness onto others, then one has fallen into step with the demonic. Judgment and a critical and negative attitude toward others springs out of an inflated opinion of oneself in most instances. The angelic seldom speaks of its own perfection. Even Jesus told those who called him good to say this of God alone. The angelic as messengers of God have the same spirit. When individuals exalt themselves, there is need to discern the reason and find out what spirit they are following.

h. There is a certain quality of destructive depression that is a sure mark of the demonic. It is one thing to go through the dark night of the soul; it is quite another to fall into self-castigating and hopeless depression and darkness. Beware of those who enjoy their misery or their sickness and turn their backs on joy. The desire to suffer can issue from the destructive, warped influence of the demonic. The martyr complex, as Karl Menniger has pointed out so clearly in *Man Against Himself*, is a form of self-hate. Hate is of demonic inspiration whether it is directed against oneself or another. It is a rejection of God to hate myself, the person for whom Christ died because he loved me so. Identification with the suffering of Christ can be a negative inflation. The early Church rejected all voluntary martyrdom. If someone tries to change our attitudes by fear rather than by love, we need to use careful discernment. Fear is his infernal majesty's most frequently used instrument. Those who would seek to save or change us by making us subject to fear may well be under anything but angelic influence. Since love is of the very nature of God, those who are influenced by the angelic (his messengers) will be characterized first, foremost and always by love. Fear will be a very minor part of the repertoire. What made St. Francis of Assisi the incomparable follower of Jesus of Nazareth was the way he incarnated the spirit of love. The angels were certainly with him.

10. In order to deal with the spiritual realm we need a language of images. Ordinary conceptual language is not adequate to the task. The language of imagination, myth, folklore and the dream is necessary if we are to be able to guide people through the maze of spiritual reality, their own and that which lies outside them and impinges upon them. It is difficult to practice discernment without a knowledge of symbols and images, for these appear to be the language of the spiritual world. Let us take a look at the language of imagination.

Chapter IV
Language, Myth and Evil

If we are to deal with any subject, we must have a language which deals with it. Languages can present problems as they can constrict us and confine us to one particular point of view. Nonetheless, languages are necessary. In the West we have lost our language which deals with spiritual reality. Only one moth-eaten word is available for discussing non-physical reality, mysticism. And this word has so many different meanings that it is practically useless.

There is a language available for dealing with this world. It is the language of myth and image, of dream and symbol. Let us take a look at how this language operates. First of all let us look at the whole problem of good and evil from the outside. We will find that this will lead us to look at the inner world. Then let us briefly look at the nature of meaning in myth and story and see how myth and history are not in any way irreconcilable opposites. Then let us see the different ways in which we can react to good and evil, to the realm of the demonic and the realm of the angelic, and finally close with some conclusions that this study suggests for the difficult task of discerning good and evil in our lives.

Good and Evil in Action

The world in which we live is both kind and cruel to human beings. It is also complicated; we human beings are supported by an intricate and interrelated physical, social, and psychological environment in a way we are only beginning to know. It is only in the past few centuries as we have come to study this complex environment that we could really know the complexity and pur-

86

posefulness in it which make possible the strange product known as conscious psychic life. In reacting to this environment, we have called *good* those aspects of this total environment which help us sustain our lives, enjoy our lives, and develop them fully and creatively. But there are also elements of our human environment which appear to be anything but helpful or creative. These aspects of the world around us and within us disrupt, destroy, and hinder us in sustaining and fulfilling our existence. And then there is the inevitable problem which stands before any reflective person, that of death, which is at least the physical cessation of life. The elements of our experience which defeat and hinder us in achieving the goals we set for ourselves, we call *evil*.

Evil breaks in upon people in many ways. There are natural catastrophes which engulf us—earthquakes, fires, tidal waves, plagues, famines. There are the social evils of war and battle, of oppression by powerful and ruthless leaders; there is poverty, social condemnation, and betrayal. And then there are the more personal and intimate evils which may or may not be associated with these others. Here we find physical sickness, mental illness, and also the less dramatic and perhaps even more agonizing evils of loneliness, meaninglessness, depression, guilt and anxiety. From the point of view of experience these all seem to be of one piece.

In the sixteenth century Thomas Cranmer wrote into the Anglican liturgy a very fine summary of the more external evils; in the words of his Litany, "From lightning and tempest; from earthquake, fire, and flood; from plague, pestilence, and famine; from battle and murder, and from sudden death, Good Lord, deliver us." Internal evils did not much occupy the men of that century; these have had to wait for their full bloom in our time with our increased self-consciousness. As we have been able to conquer the more obvious evils, we have not found ourselves free. Instead, as we have brought the grosser plagues, both outer and inner, to at least temporary truce, we find ourselves flooded with a new and intangible host of evils. We certainly have not found peace. Today's litany might well add a petition such as this: "From floating anxiety and formless terror, from loss of meaning, futility and depression, from guilt and shame, from blind hate and hostility, from compulsion and neurosis, Good Lord, deliver us." Indeed, because of our very nature, the voice of a new expert, the psychiatrist, has arisen to help us deal with these evils of the latter days, and that voice and the knowledge which lies behind it will contribute much to our discussion.

As we have come to distinguish between the good and evil elements of our environment, we have inevitably come to wonder if there is not some way in which we can control those aspects of reality which threaten, hinder, and destroy us. And this hope has led inevitably to one of the most basic of all human questions about the world: What is the origin and nature of evil? What is evil and whence does it come?

There are three essentially different ways of approaching this question. The first approach with any logic behind it sees no connection between the misfortunes which happen to us, no malignant purpose or central cause from which they arise. They are products of chance. And the good, as well as the evil which happens to us, is simply the result of chance. There is no ultimate meaning or purpose to the world, good or bad. We change what we can by our own ego power, and we submit resignedly to the rest. This was the general point of view only of the skeptics in ancient times, but it has been the standpoint of most of the materialistic scientists of the present era. Indeed it has become the basic ground upon which popular thinking is founded today.

The second point of view is difficult to make relevant to modern people because the presuppositions upon which it is based are not understood in our time. It comes from a period more optimistic about the world we live in and about human nature and human abilities and powers. It was the product of a more settled time. According to this point of view, good and evil apply only to people and their behavior. The universe itself is morally neutral, grinding on in its own inexorable way. We humans, however, by our own reason, have the power to develop a "science" of morality from rational principles which are as certain as mathematics. Principles of right and wrong exist as logical ideas that can be discovered by the use of reason, even though they have little if any relationship to the metaphysical nature and structure of reality. Good and evil, then, are rational ideas. This was the point of view of Aristotle and of Kant,

Spinoza, and John Stuart Mill. Our modern world has become disillusioned with this point of view because it has not given us the leverage we hoped for on the evil which appears to be sweeping over us more and more.

There is a third point of view, however, which has somewhat more to offer. According to this view, ultimate reality consists of a creative, upbuilding power responsible for the development of human life, and also a power or principle, a nonphysical reality which underlies and is responsible for the manifestations of evil in the universe. Neither good nor evil happens by chance, and the powers which create them are realities with which man has direct contact. This is the point of view of all the major religions of the world, from Taoism to Islam. The powers for good and for evil are realities which can be confronted. But there are also two different views on how they are related to each other.

According to the polar view of the reality of evil, it is the necessary opposite of good. To overcome its destructive effect one must accept evil as inevitable, as a necessary part of the cosmos. This is the attitude of the East, of Buddhism, Taoism and Zen, and it has been magnificently presented to the Western world by Alan Watts in many of his books. This view leads more toward resignation and inner development than to activism. One simply accepts what is. One doesn't try to change it. It is only as evil has been seen from a different view that a serious attempt has been made to destroy its evidences outwardly. The other view of the reality of evil sees it not as a necessary part of the ultimate nature of things, but as a part which can be chained and defeated.

Most of us in the Western world have been so imbued with the idea of evil as something to be eliminated that we hardly believe the Easterner when he maintains that evil must be accepted as a part of the universe and adapted to as a part of the universe. Our Western civilization has been shaped by the hope that evil can be eliminated because it was confronted and conquered by Jesus Christ. The social worker, medical doctor, public health worker, the one working to eliminate poverty or destructive political institutions may not realize where the essential motivation comes from, but it springs from the religious idea that evil is evil and can be and should be eliminated.

This is the point of view we described in the last chapter. Human beings can stand face to face with the powers responsible for evil, and they can call upon forces greater than themselves to help in the battle against evil. Once in touch with the creative powers which seem to wish to aid human beings, people can to a large extent control and direct their own fate. Many of the greatest religions have held this point of view. It was basic to Greek religion and Zoroastrianism, and also to Judaism, Christianity, and Islam. It is also basically the idea of the religion of Marxism, as well as of the modern scientific community. By most of these people it is held unconsciously, but in the writing of C. G. Jung and his followers it has been consciously appreciated and described.

Two Kinds of Thinking and Language

It is difficult, if not impossible, to deal with and describe the powers which are at root responsible for the evil in the world by using conceptual language. Whenever one tries to understand logically why there is evil in the world, one gets into real problems and often falls into heresy as well. One can only speak to ultimate issues with stories, pictures and images. Rationality is too simplistic to deal with the complexities of spiritual reality.

The most notable reaction of human beings to good and evil is one of emotion, fear, anxiety, terror, anger, hope, joy, ecstasy or a mixture of these. Not only does rationality not give us a language which is adequate to spiritual reality, it does not have a language to express our human emotions. Here we need story and poetry, images and symbols to give some sense of what we are feeling within. Rational concepts simply don't do the job. There are two kinds of thinking, and only one of them begins to be adequate to express our inner psychic world, and the outer psychic or spiritual world which impinges upon us.

All experience is really psychic experience because being experience, as such, it is an inner and not a physical phenomenon. Some portions of it refer outward to the physical world, and yet this experience is not completely exhausted by its physical sources. There are also certain experiences which show that a person gets knowledge of the external world by other means than by sense experience. These are the experiences of extrasensory perception. In addition, there are experiences which do not refer out to the physical world, but to a psychic reality or to a realm which is not physical and which we call the non-physical or spiritual world.

Besides this, humans also use two different kinds of thinking. One kind is unconscious, pararational thinking, which is thinking through images, symbols and stories. The other kind of thinking is logical, rational thinking through concepts, ideas and definitions. This latter kind of thinking, as it developed among the Greeks in the sixth century before Christ, has proved very fruitful in dealing with those experiences which come to us from the outer world. It has been practically the creator of modern science which has utterly changed our modern world and gives us power over that outer world. But this thinking has not given us the means of controlling that power, and so the world it has created around us is threatened with destruction, just as was the Greek world of which Thucydides wrote. As this kind of thinking has become more and more successful, it has spread the deep foundations for a new world-view. Probably the most unquestioned assumption is that there *is* no other reality and no other kind of thinking except logical thinking. Perhaps this view was necessary for the development of modern science, but has become a prejudice that needs careful evaluation.

There *is* another kind of thinking which has proved more fruitful in dealing with the other world of experience which is the non-physical world. This is symbolic thinking which is thinking through images. This thinking seems to flow through the individual and is not consciously directed by him/her. It is the communication of art and literature, of mythology, and also of the dream, which in reality is the individual nightly myth of each of us. These are not chaotic productions. Even dreams, it has been shown, flow in patterns which are simply concealed by the usual piecemeal experience of them. Symbolic thinking seems to come from some center of purpose within us of which we are not aware, not from the ego center with its logic or from the outside physical world. It deals with a reality of which we are not usually conscious. Myth, then, is the production of this kind of thinking directed toward the non-physical realm of being.

Only in recent years has mature rational thought been turned toward these productions of the unconscious, the artistic, literary and mythological productions. In those branches of psychology which have not been prejudiced by a materialistic bias, there has been conscious study of mythology, dreams, and artistic creations. This study has led to the realization that mythology and dreams have tremendous depth of meaning, meaning which may well hold the key to man's modern predicament. Here we are seeing the attempt to assimilate rationally and to understand consciously not only the reality of the non-physical world, but also its wisdom. This wisdom reaches expression through the non-rational production of the myth, the dream, and associated phenomena. This scientific study reaffirms that through myth and story, meanings are expressed and communications are established which are difficult or impossible through more logical means. The one who would deal with either the inner psychic world of emotion and feeling or the world of spiritual reality which lies outside the psyche must learn to use the language of myth and story. If one is to discern human emotions and the impact of spiritual reality, one will need to develop a facility in the use of this language.

The Language of Imagery

Myth, story and symbol give us a language to describe our encounters with the vast realm of spirit, both good and evil, and our reactions to it. These ways of communicating are tools and give us a language to distinguish, classify, and deal with non-physical reality, just as the symbols and formulas of chemistry help us work with the physical elements. Myth and imagery can become the language of the psychic, the non-physical world. When the psyche speaks out of its depth in dreams, it usually uses the symbols and pictures of dreams. Thus, the understanding and use of the myth and story are very practical matters in a time when men and women are harassed by a great many external and internal evils which they cannot understand rationally and with which they seem to be powerless to deal.

For centuries now, Western people have devalued myth and imagination. They have devalued the mythology of evil in particular. They have believed that only rational thought brings true knowledge, and then only if it is based ultimately on sense experience. Thus when depth psychology, in the early 1900's, began to draw some strange conclusions about the patterns in people's dreams, mythology had to be studied again and revalued.

Dr. Jung, taking up where Freud's original work stopped, laid the intellectual foundation for taking myth seriously. In addition he wrestled with the problem of evil as few others of his time. Jung was able to do so because he could draw on a sophisticated philosophical point of view along with his vast experience of the actual workings of the disturbed human psyche. He also had worked on his own inner struggle and added to his extensive study of mythology. In addition to his scientific writings for the medical profession, in his autobiography, *Memories, Dreams, Reflections*, what he discovered is told with a candid honesty and a profound self-knowledge which are rare in our time. Father David Burrell has discussed the importance of Jung in developing a language of the soul in his book *Exercises in Religious Understandings*.

In *The Other Side of Silence* I have described in some detail how one can learn to use the language of images. This is not the place to go over that material again, but rather to call attention to the fact that all of us use stories and images to express ourselves. This is a legitimate kind of language and communication and one that any person dealing with human beings in their perplexity can learn. For convenience we shall from this point on use the word myth to signify this whole class of language, story, folklore, symbol, image and dream.

The Meaning of Myth

If we are to understand what myth is, we must first of all see what myth is not. For several hundred years most Western men and women have been looking at myth rationally, quite certain that it was a poor attempt to be something which it is not. The Western mind has become so involved in a particular kind of consciousness that it gets boxed like an IBM machine in which facts breed little facts in our effort to be purely logical, purely rational and purely scientific. These circuits dealing with myth need to be shut down and something new needs to be fed in.

At one extreme is the view that myth is pure entertainment. We should have little trouble agreeing that *this* is not all that it is. Whether we listen to the ancients, or to Shakespeare or Goethe or to a modern like James Albee in his "Virginia Wolfe," there is something in addition to pure diversion. But this something is not just objective fact or analysis. It is not difficult to see that myth has its own way with facts, but it has made no great additions either to concrete history or to scientific knowledge of the world. It is not primarily a way of providing the pre-scientific mind with a ready-made cosmology. It is not a primitive attempt at science.

And so a third way of looking at myth springs up. If it is not always meant to amuse and create joy, and it fails to put out very good textbook knowledge, it must have some purpose. The myth must be a purposeful embroidering of fact in order to glorify the social order and support established ritual. Isn't this a somewhat dangerous inflation? Because we cannot find our own way of thinking represented, we impute conscious deception to the mythmakers, some of them, from Plato on down, among the world's greatest thinkers. Western thinking only reveals how set it has become in the rationalistic and materialistic world-view by reasoning like this. It is difficult to conceive of anything different from this.

Myth refers to something quite different from the rational and material worlds. Actually, mythology, according to this view, is a kind of communication. Its symbols, images and stories convey descriptions of psychic or non-physical reality which neither sense experience nor rational concepts can describe. Therefore, mythology makes a profound impression upon both the originator and the hearer of the myth. The final decision as to whether a story is in reality a myth must be decided by the impact that it makes. Real myth has a spontaneous quality about it which strikes deep and profoundly into the psyche which is open to it. Real myth however can usually be distinguished from allegory. Allegory is a consciously contrived story in which an outer situation, political or social, is portrayed point by point in symbolic language. Some stories contain elements of conscious allegory as well as myth. *Gulliver's Travels* is a typical example of social allegory, as are parts of *Alice in Wonderland*. The stories of Pandora's box and the dying and rising god are typical examples of myth.

Myth and History

It will be noted that there is nothing in this definition of myth to separate it from history. This is intentional, for myth is not the opposite of history; it is merely different from history. In fact there is nothing in the nature of myth which limits it to human imagination alone or keeps it from being embodied in outer events. It is logical and quite possible for myth to be expressed in history. The same reality which breaks forth in the images and stories of people's inner life can also be expressed in historical events. Thus one can speak of an event as being both historical and mythological.

The student can hardly fail to see mythological elements in the death of President Kennedy, in which the hero myth was acted out in actual events. The same pattern, greatly magnified, was expressed historically in the assassination of Abraham Lincoln on Good Friday, 1864. This is also the pattern which is most fully seen in the crucifixion of Jesus of Nazareth at the beginning of our era. In my book, *Myth, History and Faith*, I have elaborated the parallels at some length. One of the best statements on the relation of history and myth is found in C. S. Lewis' edition of Charles Williams' *Arthurian Torso*. These two writers have done so much to renew and revive the place of story in theology. They have written that myth is a pattern of reality which can be expressed either in human imagination or in history.

Some myths do better in describing the nature of nonphysical reality than others do. This is not the place to describe the history of these different myths in detail. In *Myth, History and*

Faith I have described some of these myths by which people live. Human beings have had all sorts of stories about the basic nature of the universe in which we live. How they view the world has an important effect upon how they manage their lives in that world. If people believe that this world is essentially a purely physical one and the human spirit is an illusion, this will influence behavior. Likewise if people believe that at the center of the universe is a being, a god, a reality which is either ambivalent or vindictive, this too will have an input into our way of living. If we see matter as the source of evil and sexuality as something which drags more spirit into matter, this will shape our ways of action and reaction. If human beings believe that all evil is a necessary part of a yin/yang sort of universe and should be assimilated, this view will give directions for living. How one views the world will determine how one behaves.

If, however, we believe the Christian myth as the best description of the basic nature of reality, then this will determine to a large extent how we live our lives. I believe that this basic Christian story is the nearest approximation to the nature of ultimate reality that we have. It states that the center of reality is love, a loving being, who wishes to relate to us and not absorb us into himself or into infinite mind. Something in that universe rebelled and broke away from his love and tried to drag us human beings into rebellion. It can be defeated and has been defeated by the death and resurrection of Jesus the Christ. As we stay in close relationship with the Risen and victorious Christ who is essentially related to the source and center of love, we can survive and come to wholeness.

Real acceptance of such a point of view has innumerable consequences as to how we map out our journeys through life. We will want to have a close relationship with the source and center to keep on the track. We will be interested in rituals and inward turnings which open the doors to this saving God. We will realize that if we are consistent, we will try to express the same kind of love to others that he has given us. We will find that kindness, compassion and outreach to others will be important values and actions. Indeed our basic story of the universe determines the values we have and hold and upon which we act.

Most human beings are not totally consistent in the pictures and stories which they hold concerning the world. They often hold one point of view with the head and another with the heart. They may believe with their heads that they are Christians and that they want to follow this pattern, but in their hearts they may be afraid and fear that God is really a tyrannical oriental despot who wishes to strike them down. It is difficult to facilitate human beings in unscrambling their crazy actions unless one can listen to their stories and value them. Then one can be useful to others in aiding them to sort out their stories and their actions which are related to these stories. This is discernment. Discernment requires of us an ability to value the importance of a person's story and to listen to it and reveal to that person the implications that this story has for his or her life. People's stories reveal who they are and where they are going. The discerner is an expert in understanding stories and myths, and in relating them to the totality of experience, including experiences of ecstasy like slaying in the spirit.

The Reality of Evil

The myth or the story I am suggesting as the most adequate description of the universe is the Christian one. It affirms that there are two poles of spiritual reality, a good one, the Triune God, and an evil one, Lucifer or Satan. The story affirms that evil wreaks havoc upon men and women outwardly and inwardly. Both poles can be experienced as one turns inward. Both realities are terribly real, and neither one can be ignored without destruction. It is often the reality of the evil pole which drives us to find the protection of the saving one. Few people are so holy or God-attuned that they seek God just for the sake of knowing him. Bonhoeffer's idea of a religion, where human beings sought God just because they wanted to, is a beautiful ideal, but doesn't show a very realistic assessment of the extent of a human's need.

My experience is that we human beings are not able to survive without God's help. The Evil One is more deeply rooted and entwined in our lives than we ordinarily realize. This one—who took advantage of the freedom God gave the spiritual reality he made and rebelled with his legion of angels—still is

hard at work, and successfully. Berdyaev remarked in his autobiography that looking back over the first forty-five years of
the twentieth century he often wondered if the powers of darkness were not smarter than the powers of light. Why is there
such a problem with discerning evil and rejecting it?

One of the reasons for confusion about evil and good is the
fact that we humans do have different reactions and different
results from our interaction with both good and evil. Good
which is part of God does not always feel good and comfortable
to us. Likewise Lucifer sometimes appears as an admirable hero
much as he appears in the pages of Milton's *Paradise Lost*. We
have four quite different reactions to good and evil.

The first and most sought-after experience is the experience
of the divine which is totally good. It may reach us when we are
in darkness, confusion or just out of the blue, and we know that
this is the ultimate power, that we are cared for, that we are
loved and that all will turn out right in the end. Such an experience can come as the very culmination of our struggling in this
direction. Often it comes when we reach out in genuine need.
We seem plucked like the brand from the burning. We have been
touched by the very heart and center of things, and it was good.
The very experience gives meaning to the word *good*. About this
experience there is no doubt, but most people have experiences
of this kind only a few times in their lives. There is no question
about this kind of experience, although some people need
encouragement to believe that what they experience is true.

Sometimes we are touched by the same reality, and the
experience is anything but pleasant. We are bending in another
way. We do not want to grow up, but the good seems to force us
to be what we don't particularly want to be. In fact it seems evil,
feels evil. I have discovered that even neurosis may often be the
hand of God tripping us up so that we cannot run away or get
into worse difficulty. If its meaning is not discovered, however,
the very obstruction can destroy us. Sometimes the good tests us
or gives us more than we believe we can handle.

From the human point of view this very experience of good
can appear completely evil. I personally resent the fact that the
way of Christ is only a way and not a safe and final destination. I
get so lost at times that I need help in discerning that I may be

causing some of my own problems. I may simply be rebelling at the task of joining my angel and animal sides together in harmony. I want to be either angel or animal and not both at the same time. I don't like the way things are and react against them. I don't like having to deal with my animalness and see that it is good. I don't like being humble. In this case good appears like evil to me.

On the other hand there are many evil experiences which undoubtedly precede growth and consciousness. Augustine refers to the *felix culpa*, the happy sin. Usually unless we sometimes fall into some sins and folly, we can forget how ugly they are and how much the deepest in us longs for something more and better. Sometimes trying to be perfect (in the sense of flawless rather than whole) can lead one to repress instinctual evil and fall into the worse sin of spiritual pride. Paul acknowledged that we ought not go out of our way looking for these growth experiences, however. This compounds the evil with a spiritual deceit.

In the story of the garden of Eden, the whole of human consciousness came through the serpent, as man began to struggle and work at living. Edens seldom produce utopias in which people grow and develop. It is very difficult to distinguish between the evil caused by good and the good caused by evil. Creative living requires a delicate balance between the two. There is not so much difficulty, however, in discerning raw, primal evil.

There is a naked evil in the world of spirit upon which we must keep an eye. All that one can do is avoid it as best one can or invoke the Christ to stand between oneself and it. One can meet this evil in psychic experience, naked destructive evil which drives a person to suicide or evil which is met more outwardly in terminal cancer, the idiot child, the psychotic breakdown, the calamitous war, the Nazi concentration camp, the tidal wave. There is evil which springs out of sheer self-centeredness described in Charles .Williams' *Shadows of Ecstasy* and *Descent into Hell.*

There is also the evil to which some people dedicate themselves. This takes as much discipline and effort as following God, with far less results. From this kind of dedication the Black Mass and most of black witchcraft spring. Hard as it is to believe, some men have made such a dedication of themselves and have had as numinous experiences of darkness and evil as others have had of God. One suspects something of this sort in the Manson family.

Faith is not a belief that there is a realm of the spirit which influences life—this is a fact. Faith is rather the conviction that neither physical, material evil nor its inner spiritual source will be able to stand against the forces of good. It is the conviction that after evil has done its best on the cross, there is still the resurrection and a new level of being. Strangely, when evil is indeed faced and overcome, there is usually a fresh burst of consciousness and life.

Dealing with Evil

As we consider the complexity of human beings and the complexity of the spiritual and physical world in which we live, the need for discernment becomes more and more clear. Often we are blinded by our own darkness, and we need the help of others to clarify where we are and where we are going. What suggestions do I have to offer? Obviously I can only offer summary suggestions culled from the spiritual classics, from the wisdom of depth psychology and from my own experience. What the religions of humankind have spent countless words and time describing can hardly be dealt with adequately by one person, no matter how remarkable his/her experience—and mine has had limits, thank goodness. But before we end such a discussion, it must be realized that talking about evil is no more helpful in controlling it than reasoning about neurosis. While our concepts about evil can determine our very lives, they do not control or defeat evil itself.

1. Thus, in the first place, evil must be accepted as real and consciously faced and dealt with. If one does not do this, the actual powers of evil fall back into the unconscious, and from there they operate without interference. They result in projections upon others, and the consequent social disruptions range from neighborhood squabbles to global war. They can strike one in physical illness, and with nameless anxieties and depressions.

Unconsciousness, as Jung has said, is evil *par excellence*, the primal human sin, and it is the moral duty of each of us to become as conscious as we can, to differentiate good from evil as best we can, and to deal with evil rather than acting in its bondage.

Of course it is dangerous to deal with evil, either inwardly or outwardly. One may be overcome and destroyed, but the chances of destruction are often better on the do-nothing side. "This is . . . to say that anyone who is destined to descend into a deep pit had better set about it with all the necessary precautions rather than risk falling into the hole backwards."[1] These last are Jung's words, and pastoral experience adds that there is such a pit in every person which usually must be entered sooner or later.

2. It is only possible to distinguish between evil things which appear good, the good things which appear evil, and naked evil as one faces evil and sees where it falls in the spectrum between good and evil. What is not faced cannot be discerned. And when we do face evil we need great discernment and wisdom. Rare is the man who does not need the discernment of another in these moments of decision. I know of no classical saint who did not have his or her confessor. It is a neat trick to differentiate between facing evil and dallying with it.

3. At this point we must be clear about the basic myths upon which we operate. If indeed we have accepted at some deep, unconscious level the myth that evil resides in matter and sexuality, we may reject our animalness, our physicalness as evil without even knowing it. There is more of this Gnostic myth in Puritanism and Jansenism than we often think, and these have had an incredible influence on modern Christianity, Catholic and Protestant, and *not for good*. One cannot change one's behavior until one renounces this myth.

4. In order to know where one is in regard to evil, one needs to keep a close watch upon one's outer and inner life. What one does is a better indication of what one deeply believes and follows than what one thinks one thinks.

Keeping an eye on one's self through a journal is a great aid to avoiding unconsciousness. Sometimes we need to listen to what others think of what we are doing as a corrective to our blindness to our own selves. The response of others to us can often reveal much about ourselves to us.

Inwardly we need to be able to express the myths that we live by and determine which of these we wish to follow and which we wish to discard. Then we need to discern how we are doing in our attempt to live by that story we have chosen. In order to do this we need first of all to take some time and reflect upon how we view ourselves. We may also find listening to our dreams very helpful, for they are the stories which rise spontaneously from the depth of ourselves when our conscious controls are off. We can also allow our imaginations to move and speak to us in the images which arise, or perhaps we can allow some passage of scripture or story to touch the imagination and stir the depth of us and so reveal to us that we are in the place that the story describes.

5. If we would offer any real help to another who is seeking to discern between good and evil, we must first of all bring an attitude of compassion and total lack of judgment and condemnation. Without this no one with any sense is going to reveal the depth of a troubled soul. There is so much condemnation from the world and from one's self that one needs no more of that. Only as the condemnation is lifted and one can look at what is actually within can the task of restoration begin. In my experience most people are condemning themselves often for the wrong things and what appear to be lesser faults.

Likewise if one is going to help in discerning a way out of difficulty for others, one must be able to listen to the others' stories, to listen to their imaginings, their dreams, their fantasies. This takes time and steadfastness. There is nothing worse we can do to those whom we would like to help than to listen to them for a while and then cut them off. Nothing is more destructive.

In order to listen without pushing our story on another, it is necessary that we know our own story consciously and realize that others have different stories, different variations of the same myth. I must know my own inner imaginings if I am to offer wise discernment to another who has sought me out. My task is to help others live their stories, not to push mine upon them.

6. Naked, essential evil can seldom be faced and dealt with other than imaginatively. One can fight its outer evidences outwardly, and this is a necessary part of the program, but if one is

to deal with that which is responsible for both the outer evil and inner evil, this can usually be done only inwardly and mythologically. Seldom can one deal simply with anxiety or depression, with futility or isolation until one turns these vague feelings into images. Doing this gives us something with which we can wrestle. Then through the use of creative imagination one can begin to cope with this reality. Imagination makes the invisible world visible so that it can be confronted. Most of the religions of mankind have provided rituals which have given mythological methods of dealing with evil. Often dramatic tragedy is a secular method of facing evil and cleansing oneself from it, as Aristotle suggested. It is in this case a real catharsis.

When one believes the basic mythology of a faith, these ritual actions actually are effective and deliver one from evil. Those who believe, for example, in the confessional are actually delivered from their guilt. But when a living religion is no longer alive in individuals, then one must make one's own mythology, one's own religion, and this is no easy undertaking. As people allow their own mythology to flow from the depths of themselves, they find the same age-old images and patterns rising up out of the unconscious. These are just as awesome and terrifying as they were to the people who first recorded such encounters.

This is more than most men can undertake. The story Jung tells of his confrontation with these realities in his own life forms the most gripping chapter of his autobiography. I have described at some length a method of dealing meditatively with evil in my book *The Other Side of Silence*. There is another dimension of reality which can be met as one turns away from total preoccupation with outer common, accepted physical reality. Adam Smith in *Powers of Mind* describes how experimenters in sensory deprivation discover such a world even when they are not looking for it.

7. If one is to face evil, either in a church or alone, one must summon all the courage of which one is capable. This is the way of the hero, as all genuinely religious people reveal when they speak of times of testing and struggle with darkness. Joseph Campbell, for example, has let the old myths speak to draw a picture in depth of one who finds this way, and Tolkien describes the dogged, persistent, patient toughness of his mythical

"hobbit" which enabled him to stand against the forces of evil and conquer in the end. These are stories of the heroic undertaking of real religion which confronts the realities of evil. Superficial religion may be easy, but the way of a living religion takes fortitude, both intestinal and intellectual. One of the facts which convinces me of the reality of Pentecostal religion is its very emphasis on the experience of testing and trial which follows the initial experience of tongues.

8. One's victory is never won without suffering and sacrifice. Sacrifice has nearly lost its meaning in our time. If one is to win the victory against evil, one must be willing to give up or abandon certain valuable parts of one's life. The genuine good must be sacrificed if the better is to be achieved, and pain and suffering are always involved, or it is not sacrifice. One must know the evil by feeling; thus suffering is often required of the hero, even at times when he/she is not called on to sacrifice consciously.

The way of the cross is a bleak mythological and spiritual reality, but those who do not go upon it seldom overcome evil. If this does not seem fair, I agree entirely; but it is not a question of fairness, but of reality. Human beings who face the "dark night of the soul" do not need to wear chains or hair shirts. Facing the evil within gives all the asceticism one needs. This kind of religion does not just satisfy human need and pacify and tranquilize it. Bonhoeffer was right in rejecting that as a brand of "religiousness." One may get onto this way through need and may be comforted, but the smooth easy road soon turns into a steep and demanding mountain trail. Pietistic wish-fulfillment is far different from this kind of religion. Dealing with the inner life does not, however, inevitably lead to pietism. Frankly, I would have made life easier for myself, and at least a few friends, if I had been God, but I wasn't given the opportunity. Those who demand of God a few jiggers of wish-fulfillment to offset every dash of bitters have probably made a mistake and gotten up to the wrong track.

9. Every hero who continues on finds his places of rest. There are resolutions, as in the book of Job, when Job's struggle with suffering and evil is solved as God speaks out of the whirlwind. There are moments of enlightenment and bliss

which make the whole undertaking worth it. On the other hand, anyone who fears the end of the process when there is no more challenge can certainly relax. This process does not happen once and for all, but continues on again and again. As soon as one resolution is accomplished, the same dialectic process begins once again. There is no measuring the unfathomable depths to which the human psyche can penetrate as it deals with mythological evil and goes the way of the mythological hero.

The basic human problem is the problem of evil. How can we differentiate evil from good and deal with the evil which co-exists in human experience as one pole of spiritual reality? It is certain that people are seldom able to deal with evil unless they use the faculty of the imagination and mythology. Reason falls short. Reason either leads one to take evil too seriously and to become rationally subservient to it, or else one is led to deny the existence of evil and thus to become unconsciously subservient to it. There is no rational escape from the painful mythological encounter. But, as the Christian myth puts it in unmistakable terms (on this level as well as in terms of eternal life), out of this encounter and struggle come life and renewed energy. Or, as Jung once expressed: "These talks with the 'Other' were my profoundest experiences; on the one hand a bloody struggle, on the other, supreme ecstasy. They were an annihilating fire and an indescribable grace."

We have seen the reality of evil and the diverse human reactions to it. We need to look now at how evil and good operate within the human life. This requires a conscious and explicit psychology, a statement about the structure and complexity of the human psyche or soul.

Chapter V
Psychology, Religion and Discernment

Psychology and religion have not always been comfortable bedfellows. Some of the reasons for this were sketched out in Chapter III. At the beginning of the twentieth century, psychology separated itself away from philosophy and became an experimental science. Those who carried this movement through its first phases were saturated with the rational materialism of the nineteenth century. They had no place for spirit, soul or religion. One can hardly blame them, for religious and philosophical thinking hadn't contributed much to psychology as a science. There has been little fellowship or harmony between psychological thought and theology for some time.

This situation need no longer continue. Robert Oppenheimer was prophetic when he spoke to the American Psychological Association in 1955. He pleaded with psychologists not to base their psychological thinking on models of reality drawn from nineteenth-century physics which physics had abandoned. No one has shown the new frontiers in psychology better than Dr. Alan McGlashan in *Gravity and Levity*. The tragedy is that theologians have on the whole either accepted the conclusions of secular psychologists as gospel or have reacted with narrow-minded anti-psychologizing which denies any value to psychological thought. There is another alternative which I have pointed out in *Healing and Christianity*. The alternative is the hypothesis which I have suggested on page 39 with the diagram and have spelled out in greater detail in Chapter III.

This is not the place to give all the evidence for taking this view of nature and human nature seriously. I have done that in *Encounter with God* and other books. Our task here is rather to see the implications of this view of human beings for dealing with evil and for discernment. We shall first of all look at the stages through which humankind passes in the course of a life. We shall then take a look at my own experience of discovery in thirty years of coming to be known to myself and of my relationship with the Risen Christ.

The Stages of Life

The enthusiasm with which Gail Sheehy's *Passages* has been received is an indication of the new interest in the variety of stages of life that we human beings live through in one lifetime. C. G. Jung had pointed to this same truth in the 1930's with a chapter called "Stages of Life" in *Modern Man in Search of a Soul*. Erik Erikson has elaborated in a series of books these various stages through which we pass from the cradle to the grave. Lawrence Kohlberg has also sketched out six stages of moral development.

The point of view we have suggested as that of Jesus and the early church fits in well with this dynamic view of human nature as the growth and development toward the ultimate goal of eternal life. If one is going to aid one's self or another person in passing from stage to stage, it is necessary to be clearly aware of the various stages of the trip we call life. What is adequate behavior in one stage of life is not adequate in another. The task one must perform at one time in a life span can only be performed earlier or later at a high cost. Whether one is teaching or counseling, being a parent or just listening to a friend, it is wise to be able to discern in which stage the individual is and to react appropriately to the person in that stage.

Keeping in mind the diagram on p. 39 we see that the individual who comes into the world is represented by the cut-off triangle on the left side of the line. New-born children have almost no sense of their own personality. The two-year-old who is beginning to talk refers to him/herself as "the baby." It is difficult for the child before five to distinguish between the inner and the outer worlds, between material and non-physical experiences. Many children have imaginary playmates who are often seen as real physical beings. Adults get nervous if children continue talking about their inner worlds as physically present after they are five. William Blake was beaten by his parents because he insisted that he could see spirits in trees and bushes. The child, just like the psychotic, is in touch with an inner world and often fails to distinguish this inner world from the outer one. The Rorschach tests of children and psychotics are therefore similar.

One of the important learning experiences of children is to learn that there are different worlds. There is a physical world which is both fun and dangerous. There is also a spiritual one which contains "bogey men" as well as angels. Children are very open to spiritual reality and can be taught a great deal about this world. They are like tender, sensitive, living plants. They can be trained so they are open to relating to God as love at the center of reality or closed to this idea because of the way that human beings have treated them. The child needs warmth and understanding and love if he/she is going to be open to those elements in the universe. Baron von Hügel's study of the life of Alfred Lyall in *Religion and Agnosticism* is a penetrating discussion of this truth. One reason for social action directed toward the elimination of poverty and slums is that children brought up in these conditions can be so crippled by these conditions that it is almost impossible for them to believe that there is any goodness or love in the universe. And of course there is the reason of compassion also. No one should live under those conditions, and certainly the children did not create them.

Just because the human being must learn to deal with often unpleasant physical reality, there is no reason why one must be convinced that the spiritual one does not exist. The problem is that Western children are grafted into a culture which has little or no place for spiritual perceptions. Probably something of the same thing happened even in the ancient world, for Jesus said: "Except you become as little children you shall in no wise enter into the kingdom of heaven." Children for Jesus were a model of openness to spiritual reality. As small children grow they can learn to distinguish between different aspects of reality rather than being taught to deny one part of it entirely. Children can pass from this early childhood stage to the next at any time from three to seven or eight. In dealing with children religiously it is crucially important to discern where the child is. I know of no better explanation of the life of the young child than Frances Wickes' classic *The Inner World of Childhood*. It presents the depth and complexity of this stage of life with clarity and sympathy and gives a base for understanding the next stage as well. It also gives adults an understanding and insight into their own childhood development.

Once one has developed a center of personality so that one can distinguish between the inner and the outer worlds and begin to take the outer one seriously, the child is said to have begun to develop an ego and is ready to move on to the next stage of development. The way that the word *ego* is used in this book has no moral connotations. The ego is simply the stable "I-ness" which one must develop if he/she ever is going to be able to cope with either the inner or outer world. If one does not develop this center or ego to a condition of strength, one is condemned to the shadow life of mental illness or to remaining an autistic person. Without some consistency and love in one's environment the child seldom passes out of stage one.

The next stage of childhood is one of learning the knowledge, morals and values of one's culture and assimilating the knowledge which is necessary to survive in our complex modern world. A culture carries the collective wisdom of a society and it is essential to have this. Children are greedy learners unless a stupid, rigid and *undiscerning* school system turns the torrent of desire for learning into a trickle. Children from seven to eleven shouldn't spend too much time developing their own ideas, but rather they should be given the time to take in the world. What is given to animals in instincts, human children must learn during these years.

Children come into the world with a potential structure in their ways of looking at or perceiving the world. Early training reinforces this pattern so that they come to have different ways of learning. If one is going to help a child learn, one must discover (or discern) what type structure that young person has. Unfortunately our society and our school system give almost exclusive priority to intuitive and thinking type functions. The child who is primarily interested in feeling, which in Jungian terms is the sense of evaluating, or in sensation, which is the capacity to perceive and deal adequately with physical reality, is given little appreciation or stimulation. Interesting studies have shown that children who are primarily oriented to using and developing sensation are the first ones to drop out of school.

It is believed that children are most likely born with a tendency toward a definite type-structure and should be helped to develop what they already are. It is like right and left handedness; one will never be as good in using the other functions as one is in using the ones with which he/she was endowed by birth.

If children are to be helped to grow in their learning and be able to share their gifts with others, they must be appreciated for what they are. Nearly every educational research study which has investigated the question has also come up with data showing that children learn more easily and more deeply in a situation where they are treated with love and compassion and warmth. The warm environment stimulates growth whether it is in the home, the church or the school. This stage of life is the time for adapting to their culture or acculturation.

When a child is not learning we need discernment to see what has gone wrong. It may be that we are trying to force the child to be something that does not fit his/her personality structure. It may be that the child needs more understanding and warmth. It may be that some early trauma has disrupted the child's life. It may be that some physical injury has retarded the child. Or the child may be carrying the unresolved darkness and unfaced evil of the parents. Deciding what is wrong is hardly possible without a knowledge of the nature of the child and his or her stages of development. Physical punishment is certainly *not* the answer, as a large number of research studies show. Parents need to develop their own powers of discernment and be willing to ask for and accept expert advice on this subject.[1]

Adolescence and Adulthood

Some time between eleven and sixteen years of age another stage develops. It comes about the time of puberty. Young men and young women then begin to be more interested in their peer groups than in their family units. There is a stirring to separate out from the home, to revolt against parental values, to make intimate and sexual bonds of their own outside the family. In nearly all conventional societies (and I use that term rather than the pejorative word primitive) there were once initiation rites to help the young men and women step through this period of transition. We in the West have so lost the sense of ritual and ceremony that we provide almost nothing to help young people through this stage. For this reason, among others, many young people have a real time of crisis during this period.

It is impossible to deal creatively with this age group unless we treat each young person as an individual growing toward autonomy and independence. This poses a problem for the counselor since the person from twelve to eighteen (or twenty-one in some states and countries) is legally under the parents' control. During the years of childhood most children go along with their parents and accept the parents' religion and other values with enthusiasm. They support their parents and their ideas and values with their friends. Now a real change takes place. The religious practices of parents are rejected and parental values are questioned. This period is difficult for parents and yet is necessary for adolescents to go through if young people are to come to their own ability to function independently or to autonomy.

Sometimes young people do very foolish things just to show that they are free and independent. A person cannot really "own" a value system as his or her own unless the person has first of all rejected the old one and worked out his/her own. Sometimes the old one is identical to the new, but through the struggle the person has made it his/her own.

What discernment it takes to guide young people through this period. The church was wise in providing the idea of godparents, as every child and young person needs someone close to them outside of the family. The young person's revolt puts the parent in a double bind. Parents and teachers can be wrong if they resist this movement toward self-determination and also wrong if they go along with it and cooperate too enthusiastically. Parents must know where they stand and know their own point of view so that young people can revolt against it if necessary without being rejected by the parents.

One minister friend has told me of an experience with his daughter. She had been very active in his church and then at about fifteen declared that she no longer believed in God and did not wish to go to church. The minister reasoned that if he had not laid a firm foundation by fifteen, he couldn't force it upon her now. He told her that she didn't have to go to church if she didn't wish to. And she didn't until she became interested in a young man and brought him into the church. Then they were married and had children and became very intelligent and active members of the church. How wrong he might have been to stand against this adolescent revolt.

If one can stand it, most young people pass through this stage. They learn the importance of responsibility, intimacy, autonomy and self-sufficiency. They come to the point where they are no longer led by their peer groups, but by their own values which have gradually emerged. They select a profession and move out into the world as adults. Someone has remarked that one of the greatest values of going away to college is to get the young people out of the homes and keep them in a relatively safe environment until they grow up. Adolescence often extends into the early twenties and even beyond, and some people never pass out of it. Charles Reich's *The Greening of America* and Andrew Weil's *The Natural Mind* give a good picture of the revolt of youth and their search for new values. Let's face it, sometimes the parents' values are not right. Sometimes the parents have been taken in by a materialistic culture and do not see how inconsistent it is with the religious values which they profess. Dealing honestly with one's children can help parents grow up too.

Young adulthood is a time for establishing oneself in the world. It is the time for marriage and intimacy, getting on with one's job, of establishing oneself in the community, the church and a circle of friends. In many cases it is not a time of deep inner searching, nor should that be encouraged unless the individuals are seeking it on their own without outside encouragement. Like the latter part of childhood, it is a time of assimilation and growth and development of potential, a time of challenge. Now, however, it is assimilation according to one's *own* pattern and not just according to that of parents and teachers.

There was a time when only a few young adults found this stage a period of doubt, uncertainty, questioning. Jung in his article on the stages of life suggests that few people turn inward for meaning until after thirty-five. But times have changed. I do not know what has caused the change, whether it is the drug culture or the breakup of Western materialism or youth's intuitive grasp of the physicists' doubts about the certainty of their laws or the fiasco of the Vietnamese war. But I find that many college-age young adults are forced into dealing with the depth of themselves, searching for meaning, reaching out to relate to spiritual reality. Twenty years ago these were the problems of the person from thirty-five to fifty. During that period many people have achieved many of their goals. They have had their families. They have attained their position in the world. Crossing the halfway point in life, from thirty-five to fifty, the question of death rears its ugly head and the problem of meaning becomes more intense. One's children have left the nest and this creates a serious problem for women who have focused their main energy on the home.

It is difficult to put too much stress on the importance of listening to young adults, *or* older persons, if they have begun to talk about finding meaning. If one dismisses these questionings or gives pat answers to them, the great steel door clangs shut and significant relationship is over. It was hard for me to realize that many college students at twenty-one were where I was in my early thirties. I had to use all the discernment of which I was capable in order to listen and be of help to those passing through this stage earlier than I had thought possible. They have the difficulty of passing through it without the life experience or wisdom that more years might have brought them.

We shall defer our discussion of the search for meaning until the next chapter. It was to express my own struggle to find meaning and to share it that led me to write *Encounter with God*. Unless one is able to find meaning either in some social or religious group or within one's self, the years of later adulthood can be barren and bitter. Everything turns to dust and ashes in one's mouth. Boredom sets in. One may seek an increased tempo of activity to forget the meaninglessness, or one may turn to some form of distraction, to drugs or alcohol, to television or too much work. Most men and women in this situation avoid any serious encounter with themselves because they are trying to avoid the inner emptiness. Mr. Smith looks into the mirror and wonders who he is after all and then concludes that no one knows who one is.

Even if one has been closed to genuine religion since early childhood, one may be open at this time. The agnostic is not morally evil; he is starved and needs nourishment. One may turn inward at this period of life. With honesty one finds a depth and complexity in one's psyche or one's soul. At this point one either prepares for the next stage or one reacts with denial and anger, with fear and depression. The next stage consists of two phases. The first can be a golden age. It is reaping the harvest of a well-lived life. Many people can be free to do many of the things they always wanted to do. However, this phase without inner meaning can also be a disaster. The second phase is old age which leads either to despair or to eternal life.

How little society or the church does to reach out and touch the person in old age. Since most people view this period as simply approaching the end of the road, it is considered that there is nothing that can be done except to learn to "grin and bear it." A meaningful dealing with old age and death requires a meaningful use of the second stage of adulthood. If life leads in the last analysis only to the grave and dissolution back into the earth, there isn't much that one can offer. Death was even more taboo than sex until the work of Dr. Elisabeth Kübler-Ross. Her book *On Death and Dying* and her subsequent studies should be required reading for anyone dealing with the aging and the dying. These people may need companionship more than any other group, and yet we cannot creatively deal with them until we have faced our own fears of meaninglessness and death. Dealing with this group requires quite a different approach than with the other stages along the road. Responding to these individuals requires discernment and empathy, sensitivity and openness.

Some feel that this group does not seek relationship or understanding. Nothing could be further from the truth. In a church where I once served we had groups for those in the earlier stages and then realized we had nothing for the older people. A group for people over sixty-five was enthusiastically received and the questions which faced these people were discussed with a candor that would have shocked some of the younger people. Many people like these find Raymond Moody's *Life after Life* a great help in opening the door of discussion and easing away the fear of looking at death and talking about it.

We have briefly outlined six stages of life. Each requires a different kind of response and discernment. However, as one deals with people of all ages one realizes that chronological age does not necessarily determine where one is on the journey. One may face death at twelve or still be a big baby at seventy or be moving toward meaning at eighteen. Since so much depends on one's first approach to another, the importance of understanding the various stages of development and discerning where a person is can hardly be overestimated.

In addition to these stages of life through which we pass, the psyche has great depth and complexity. Let us take a depth look at the soul using a method which I have developed at length in *The Other Side of Silence*. Obviously a knowledge of this structure is necessary for discernment.

A Picture of the Soul

As a child I often wondered what the soul looked like. The way that my questions about it were answered told me that those who talked to me didn't believe that the soul actually existed or else they had a very foggy notion of its nature. As I moved into my thirties and was faced with the necessity of finding meaning, I was forced to do a lot of probing into the nature of my psyche or soul. As I continued to search out what made me tick, I found all sorts of seemingly unrelated parts of me. I certainly realized that with an inner crew like this I needed help to bring about any sort of unity in my life and my actions.

The picture of my soul which I now present came together for me toward the end of a sabbatical year when I had had more time than usual for reflection. It emerged through a series of image meditations. I am sharing the process through which these insights occurred. I hope that this may make the content more concrete and also reveal how one can use the imagination and myth when one is dealing with the non-physical world. I also wish to make quite clear that this is *my* myth and the inner figures which appeared to me were *mine*. Other people may have other figures moving within them and charging their lives with energy. Reading this story may encourage others to try to do the same thing for themselves. This is a practice which has been most helpful to me and many others with whom I have shared it.

In my fantasy I often find myself in a little cabin by the sea. This cabin sits high on a rock. On one side one can hear the pounding breakers, and on the other there is a grassy meadow which leads up to the forest and the mountains beyond. Paths and roads converge from many directions here at this rustic cabin built of rough-hewn timber. Inside are several rooms. In the largest one there is a large hearth with a log fire blazing on it. It is raining outside. One can hear the moaning of the wind and the drip of the rain from the eaves as well as the beating of the waves against the cliffs.

I am alone. I have been turning in upon myself, thinking of who I am and where I am to go from there. I am roused from my reveries by a knocking on the door. I wonder who would be out on a night like this. I light a candle and go to the door, and there by the doorway stands a youth in his early twenties or late teens. He is drenched. I welcome him in and pour a drink for him. I get him some dry clothes. He dries himself before the fire and then puts on the clothes I brought. Then he dries his own clothes before the fire. I ask him why he is there and who he is and he replies that he is a part of me and that I seem to be in the right frame of mind to relate to him.

We have only said a few more words and there is another knock at the door. Again I answer and this time find a middle-aged woman and a forlorn and bedraggled child whom she is leading by the hand. With the youth helping me we get a tub to wash the child. The woman has been well covered with a thick and heavy cloak. She has cared well for herself. She takes over as soon as she sees that the child is being cared for. She looks around for what she can find and begins to prepare a meal for all of us. By this time I am surprised at nothing. I noticed that a quick affection has sprung up between the youth and the child. I wonder if they have known each other before. And then there is another knock at the door. This time I find a young and very attractive woman; beautiful would be a better word for her. Both the young man and the child come forward to offer whatever help they can be to her.

Soon the three of them are sitting at one side of the hearth and carrying on an animated conversation. They ask how long it will be before the older woman (she is an archetypal mother) will have food ready for them. The next knock is a thunderous one. I wonder if the door will hold to its hinges. Opening it I find a soldier before me, dressed as a soldier of ancient times. He has on a helmet and a short tunic. He carries a sword. He does not push his way in. I realize that all of these people were powerless to enter without my invitation. How quickly the young woman, the maiden, runs to be of help. I can see the youth is irked. The older woman only gives the soldier an acknowledging glance. She knows him. He joins our group around the fire. He is boisterous, but not a bad sort.

I am really quite amused. I realize that I have met all of these characters before, but never have had them together and that I have needed to have them meet one another and relate. Then comes another knock. This one is imperious. As I open the door I find a man in his middle life, distinguished looking, a bit stuffy and saturnine. He has obviously ruled others and has a kingly air about him. The crew are not impressed and do not hurry to get water for his hands. They do not bow or scrape. He is one of them and so they treat him.

The next sound I hear is a light one, firm but light. I almost know whom I will find as I throw open the door. Here is the scholar, the professor, the sophist, the intellectual. He carries some books under his one arm and carries a walking stick in the other. Not too many steps behind him follows a medieval fool with his pointed hat and motley clothes. The scholar walks in and takes his place in a corner. The youth comes and takes his coat. He pays little attention to the others but buries his nose in a book almost at once. The fool, however, bounces in and creates quite a stir. He dances around and asks for some warm, dry clothes. Even with ordinary clothes he is a character. No one seems to mind his jests and even the professor in his corner is not too annoyed when he snatches the book he is reading from his hands and asks if he has anything in his head or if it is all in books.

The room is nearly filled and I am wondering how many more will seek shelter from the stormy night. There is one more knock and I usher in a large, powerful man. He is heavily built but he is lame. He carries some tools in a quiver-like container. He looks about my place and says that it is certainly time that he came as the place really needs some repair.

There are nearly enough cushions for everyone to sit down. We make a circle around the blazing fire. The older woman serves a meal of quick bread and a thick soup and there is wine. All goes well for a while until the soldier begins to make a play for the maiden, and this enrages the smith and also the youth. The child is neglected and begins to scream. He has messed his pants and no one wants to be bothered. The scholar shouts that he can't stand this crowd and perhaps he would be better off in the stormy night. No one says a thing to stop him, but he doesn't go. And none of them pay any attention to me. I realize that I cannot control this zoo by myself and I think that I had better call upon the master. Scarcely have I thought this through than he appears. I do not have to open the door to him. He is just there. Quiet, soft-spoken, warm in speech and action, he quickly brings order.

The evening under his direction becomes sort of an inner group therapy session. They all introduce themselves and each one tells how he or she happened to be there. Soon we are all in good humor and talking to one another. But something is wrong. It is flat, unreal, tasteless. I turn toward the master and ask what is lacking. He laughs and says: "You have been so noisy that you have not heard that there are others who wish to enter. Let's be quiet and listen."

This statement causes a very negative reaction. They do not want to listen, but they do, and as the noise dies down, a thumping noise is heard coming from below the cabin. The smith soon locates a trap door in the wooden floor and beneath this there is a trap door cut in the living rock upon which the cabin stands. Several of the men strain and pull and the door springs open. Sulfurous fumes billow up and out of them step seven or eight (or maybe nine) of the most horrid creatures that I have ever met.

The first of them is a Medusa-like figure with snakes for hair, bent on devouring and destroying even her own young. A black widow spider of enormous size is perched on her shoulder. Then an Aztec priest emerges with feathered head-dress and all. In one hand he carries the obsidian knife with which he has just sacrificed his sixty-seventh victim to appease the sun god and in the other hand the still beating heart of the last victim. And then a man strikes out with a whip in hand. He proudly announces he is a slave trader and asks if there are any among our group we would like to sell. His eye rests upon the youth and the maid and child. I withdraw in horror. Then the wild destructive monster, like the monstrosity of Frankenstein, appears. He lumbers in and strikes out wildly this way and that. And then there is a caricature of the smith. He holds in his hands instruments of torture which he has just invented and is eager to use.

I wonder how much more of this I can stand. Yet there are others. An idiot child, snivelling, drooling, crying. A wild destructive youth who has just pulled apart a hamster and watched it writhe in pain. There is a whore-like gunman's moll, painted, hard, and yet one who could have been beautiful. There is a mad fool who thought that he could manage anything and tried to run countries instead of amusing them, and brought horror and destruction. And last of all there is the scholar bent on making perfect plans for the conquest of the world, intelligence turned over to selfishness and power.

They advance toward us and we all shrink back, all except the master. He stands there quite unconcerned, and as they come forward he touches them one by one. I can hardly believe what I see. As he reaches out they fall to the ground and look like ashes. As this occurs a dark shadow escapes from the rubble which they become and scurries like a rat back into the hellish hole from which it came. Each time this happens, one of the original nine guests who have come into my place by the sea receives a jolt of life. At last all of our dark visitors are all so much dust and ashes and eight or nine dark shadows have slipped back into the hole which still belches smoke. At this the warrior and the smith rush forward and let the stone trap door down and then close the wooden one as well.

Long into the night we sit and talk. I learn so much. These

nine men and women who have come to my door were neutral parts of me. If they are under the direction of wholeness and harmony, the master, the Risen Christ, then they work together. If they are left alone they quarrel and cause chaos. But worst of all they can fall into the hands of the Evil One. His stratagem is to convince each one that he or she is the only valuable person within and should subject the others to him or her. Evil is most often found when a lesser good pretends to be the only good. Each of my nine guests gives me a name to help identify him or her. They have many names, but I know their Greek names best. The problem on Mount Olympus was that they each tried to operate separately.

I now see that the motherly one who called herself Demeter (the earth mother) could be the nurturing, caring, sustaining mother. But when she fell into the hands of the separating force of evil she could become the Medusa-like destroyer, devouring her own mate like the black widow spider. The child could either be the divine child like Eros himself, or else he could be the cowardly, panic-stricken idiot, betraying and forsaking those he admired the most.

The youth said that his name was Hermes. If he was related to the rest and to the powers of heaven, then he was the divine angel-like messenger of the God, inspirer, bringer of beauty and grace. Or he could become the destructive hood bent on sense-less destruction for its own sake. And the maiden whose name was Aphrodite could be like Beatrice who inspired Dante and drew him into the highest level of heaven, or else the wild, self-seeking, prostitute who would sell any man for her gain, a woman like Delilah. I realized how much I needed Ares, for that was the warrior's name. Without his strength the women and the children could never be protected. He could keep the wild forces of hell from breaking in. And yet when he was caught up by evil and in league with hell he became the destroying Hitler or Attila or Tamerlane wreaking havoc on the whole world. The older man, the kingly one, said that his name was Zeus and he could bring justice and order. When he was subservient to hell he became the oriental despot or the slave trader, using his power to own and possess others.

The fool said that he had no other name than fool. If he was related to the others and to love, he would bring the bright relief of humor. He could help us all from getting too serious, but when alone or in the hands of the Evil One he became a stupid, destructive Frankenstein's monster. I could see the two sides of Intellect. That was his name. He had no Greek name. He had only emerged in his glory in Western Europe in recent years. Some said his name was Science. He could be either the one who led St. Thomas to bring together all wisdom to his great work or he could be the disembodied head of C. S. Lewis' *That Hideous Strength* which used cold intellect to subject and dehumanize human beings. And then the lame fellow called himself Hephaestos. Under this name he was the Greek god of the forge. He could make plows and pruning hooks or he could make spears and swords and instruments of torture.

From this I am able to construct a picture of my soul. It seems to contain my own "I-ness," my ego and my nine other personalities of force. From above I am open to the infinite powers of heaven and from below to the very powers of hell which have a beachhead within my soul. Here is the diagram as I have worked it out (cf. page 122). The nine small spheres represent these inner figures for whom I have used the names which came to me within this imaginative encounter.

My task is to realize that these inner figures are not evil in themselves. Sexuality, power, childlikeness, aggression, intellect are not evil. They are not to be exercised just on their own, for their own sake, but brought into harmony with the others and brought to the victorious, loving, risen Christ. I need to realize that they can become evil when they operate alone or fall into the hands of the Dark Lord.

I need discernment if I am to see the figures who operate within my life and take control. I need wisdom to discern what powers are within me or within another. Then I can understand when these inner powers have gone wrong and lead them to the fellowship of the Christ who alone can give them their real potential. I can also help others do the same thing. Yet this help is only for those in later life who are seeking for meaning, unless one comes upon young people who have been thrown by the modern world into this inner searching.

The task of knowing these inner forces is one which most of

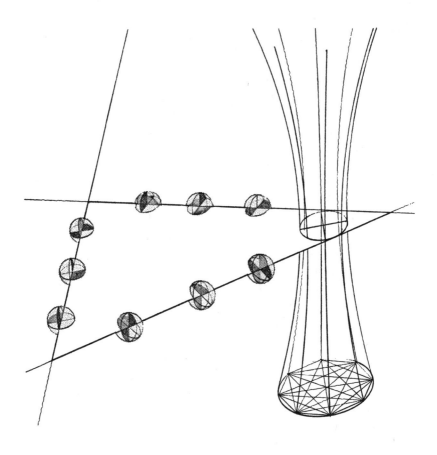

us need to keep at for the rest of our days once we have started on it. There is limitless room for growth in the potential that has been given to us. It is no wonder that we need eternal life. We can only get a start on the task even in one magnificent lifetime. I doubt if a loving God would send us back through life with as little knowledge of where we have been as we seem to have as we start this journey in childhood.

Chapter VI
Discernment in Counseling

Everyone has problems at some time or another in life. And nearly everyone sometimes needs to talk to another person outside the confines of his/her own family group. Sometimes the problems involve relationships with a member of the family and so one needs an outside objective ear. If we are open and caring we will find that people often want to talk with us and we find ourselves counselors whether we like it or not.

The suggestions which follow are intended primarily for professional counselors, teachers, social workers, psychologists, family counselors, ministers and church workers. They apply, however, just as well to any Christian who takes discipleship seriously. As we noted in the first chapter, to give encouragement, to be of service and to show kindness were seen as charismatic gifts in the early church. Even Carl Rogers, the well-known authority on counseling, is reported to have remarked that counselors are born, not made. The real pastor, whether ordained or lay, is the one who can listen to a person and then reach out with a response which has a healing and strengthening effect. Individuals who find themselves in this counseling role need to learn of the developments in the counseling field in recent years.

Over the past seventy years great strides have been made in developing methods for enabling one person to be a counselor for another. These methods aim at creating conditions through counseling so that people can approach and handle many of their most pressing problems. In this way many people have been able to resolve conflicts, to come through one crisis or another and find new energy, and even greater personal wholeness and meaning. Counseling is Christian love in action, enabling people to come to their greatest potential growth.

123

There are not enough professional counselors around to deal with the problems which human beings seem to have with themselves. The very scarcity is reflected in the fees that a good counselor commands. Anyone within the church or a part of a Christian fellowship who can listen and is willing to take the time will find someone knocking on the door. What I write in the concluding pages of this book applies equally to professional counselors and to those who find that they have a gift and that troubled human beings are using it. For the sake of simplicity I will refer to all of those who are sought out for this help as *counselors.* I shall deal with one particular area of counseling, one often experienced by lay counselors as well as professionals—the problem of meaning.

The Art of Christian Counseling

There is one human circumstance which leaves many counselors perplexed, feeling they lack either the expertise or the understanding to work with it. This is the problem of meaninglessness, the failure to find meaning and purpose in life or the loss of it. The person is stopped, bottled up; there seems to be no reason to step out into the rough and tumble of life, or even to arouse oneself to the problem. Yet this is a problem that presents itself to the counselor either masked by some symptom or reflected by a feeling that one simply does not know what can be the matter with him. Generally it is clear that nothing quite makes sense. Among the primitives this condition is known as "loss of soul," and it is my experience that it occurs very frequently among moderns who do not know what to call it.

The person suffering from this basic illness—and illness it is—can manifest a variety of symptoms. Loss of meaning can come out as depression, the so-called "simple" depression for which clinical psychology and psychiatry are able to do so little as the statistics show. It may surface as a floating anxiety, hanging like a gray cloud over the person's life and robbing one of any sense of vitality or joy. Or, the anxiety can be concretized as a specific phobia or fetish, attached to an object or action in a way that even the individual may realize is silly.

The same anxiety and fear can be expressed as anger,

through a defensive reaction to the fear; and hostility or rage may then be turned against either the outer world or inwardly. In the one case, the feelings of fear and frustration are generally acted out by hostility toward other people; and in the other, they are turned against the person himself, keeping one from functioning as one wishes. In *Man Against Himself*, Karl Menninger has brought out in detail the many ways this self-hate can interfere disastrously with a person's life. As I shall suggest, some of the common problems like alcoholism can be traced to this reaction, born out of a fear of finding oneself in a meaningless universe. James J. Lynch has pointed out the medical consequences of loneliness and loss of meaning in his important book *The Broken Heart*.

In counseling, these reactions can usually be brought into the open and understood. Once a good relationship has been established with the counselor, so that the person is more free to explore real feelings, he or she is usually able to see which feelings are based in reality, and which ones do not fit actual experience. In spite of casting blame in one direction or another, one may realize that there has been no real problem of childhood traumas or bad conditioning; that one has successfully come through any identity crisis, establishing at least an adequate self-image; and that one has been able to handle sexual conflicts quite well, and actually has a good enough relation with parents and others. Yet the problem is still there, and these common psychological problems do not account for the depression the person faces. The individual seems to be adrift, without adequate meaning to tie into. In my own counseling I have worked with quite a few people who found that their real difficulty was one of finding meaning, and that when they became aware of this, the parts of the puzzle began to fall into place.

Filling the Vacuum

Two of the major problems facing American society today suggest the need for meaning strongly at the present time. These are drug abuse and alcoholism, problems which the counselor must meet again and again. Alcoholics Anonymous and Teen Challenge are among the few really successful attempts to deal with these problems, and both of them base their efforts on an attempt to fill the vacuum of meaning in the victims' lives. Teen Challenge is described by David Wilkerson in *The Cross and the Switchblade*; it is a bid to release drug addicts by offering them the pervasive meaning of the Pentecostal group. Most of us have a superficial knowledge of AA. The story behind this amazing movement is told by Robert Thomsen in his absorbing biography of the founder, *Bill W.* The alcoholic finds release from the compulsion to drink as he finds meaning beyond his/her life.

Studies of the American Indian also suggest clearly that the increase in alcoholism among Indians has occurred whenever the traditional religion has lost meaning and there has been no other to fill the gap.[1] On some reservations the rate of alcoholism is as high as 50%. Apparently both drug addiction and alcoholism represent an escape from life which appears to have lost value and purpose for the individual.

These two are only the most striking examples of the current results of the fear of life-without-meaning. This is also reflected by the increase in chronic and psychosomatic illness, and again this fact has been recognized among the Indians. The Department of Health, Education and Welfare has been subsidizing a school for shamans, or medicine men, among the Navajos, specifically because studies have shown that mental and physical illness among the Navajos can be healed by this means (which has religious meaning to them) when medical science has been powerless to help.[2] I have seen much the same thing confirmed in my own work, along with the fact that finding meaning and value in life often, at the same time, brings a resolution of the problem of hatred and anger and hostility.

There seems to be little question that a method of finding meaning is important for those who feel that they are lacking it. And it is my suggestion that this can be provided through counseling. Christian counselors need to realize that they have something to offer which most systems of modern psychological thought do not offer, and which is needed in many of the situations they normally handle. These are the deadlocks which require faith (someone's faith in meaning and purpose beyond the individual) in order to tackle and resolve the problems presented. The counselor who cannot step into such situations with the help that is needed fails the one in need. Let us look at these questions, and then consider at what point the need is found. Later we shall suggest a method of presenting meaning to an individual.

If we are adequately equipped as counselors, then we will be prepared to meet this need. But this does not mean that we will simply try to impose our own value system or our worldview upon the person seeking help. Rather, when the situation suggests it we will be able to present the case for a meaningful universe *in what we say, in what we are and how we live.* There is no basic difference between this and one's primary task as a counselor, which is learning to listen to the person who comes without judging the person from one's own value system. In offering meaning, one is trying to help the person find a way and meaningful values.

So many do-gooders, particularly religious ones, have tried to push their moral or religious ideas (which are usually only cultural and not basic Christian or religious ideas) on those in need that we have quite naturally become afraid of this. We fail to see that there is a time and a place to help others find meaning, not by dictating it, but by letting them share with us in what we have found. At the same time, counselors need to be thoroughly aware of their own values and religious beliefs so that they will not find themselves imposing these values and beliefs upon other persons. It is an art to be able to provide meaning when this is needed and also an art to keep still when it is not.

Faith

Dr. Jerome Frank states in *Persuasion and Healing*, his fascinating study of psychotherapy and healing, that medical doctors interested in physical healing are better able to bring restoration if they understand the importance of faith to their patients. He concludes his book with these words:

> . . . faith may be a specific antidote for certain emotions such as fear or discouragement, which may constitute the essence of a patient's illness. For such patients, the mobiliza-

tion of expectant trust by whatever means may be as much
an etiological remedy as penicillin for pneumonia.[3]

In another place, Dr. Frank suggests that "anxiety and despair
can be lethal, confidence and hope, life giving."[3] He goes on to
say that up until the discovery of modern antibiotics some forty
years ago, most doctors were actually faith healers without
knowing it, for the simple reason that most of their remedies
were medically inert. Dr. Alan McGlashan has supported the
same point of view in *Gravity and Levity* where he states: "It is in
fact very difficult to cure anybody of anything by means of a
remedy in which you yourself have no faith. The successful
doctor, no less than the successful 'quack,' is the man who is
really convinced he has got something."[4] The fact that our
bodies are so responsive to trust, hope and faith should make it
easy to see that these elements are equally necessary for emotional health and a healthy adjustment to one's environment.

Yet there is little suggested in most modern schools of counseling that confidence, trust and meaning might be indispensable
factors in resolving problems. On the contrary, orthodox Freud-
ian psychotherapy has handed down to us the understanding
that we humans are equipped with only our reason to hold our
ground against the blind and unrelenting forces of the universe.
Freud's religious point of view is drawn out very clearly in *The
Future of an Illusion*. The individual faces a cold war, and must
gird himself to keep these forces—which are the Id, the death
wish, and the super-ego—balanced one against the other.
Maturity means being satisfied in a meaningless universe which
few people are really capable of enduring.

Behaviorism offers the individual, particularly the conscious
and perceptive person, no more in the way of meaning or ultimate hope. In this system, the human being is considered merely
a complex configuration of conditioned responses, with little to
look forward to or have faith in, except to be manipulated by
other people through operant conditioning. This approach can
often produce results with problems that do not involve the person's system of values. Behaviorism gives excellent results when
it is a matter of helping retarded children fit into cultural patterns. But not all of us are retarded, and if our problem is one of

finding meaning in the universe, just what can this discipline offer us? Students at Notre Dame, I find, steer clear of discussing their real problems with the behavioral psychologists, because they have no desire to be manipulated. And anyway, I doubt if one can be operantly conditioned into a sense of meaning. The conditioned pigeons don't often ask what it all means.

The existential and humanistic psychologists do consider the person more than a thing to be dealt with; they believe that meaning arises from the depth of the individuals themselves in some peak experience. But if a person looks deep within and finds no meaning, the humanistic counselor has little more to offer. In a world riddled with war and confusion and pain, there is not much to point to that will help a person who already lives with fear. If peak experiences cannot be seen as coming from any reality beyond human life, then they are not likely to give the individual a reason for overcoming fear and stepping out into life with courage.

On the other hand, what if there *is* some reality beyond the individual, something in which humans can trust? Then the counselors have a very important task. It is up to them, when a person is seeking, to help that person find a relationship with a reality which can give him or her meaning and hope. This is certainly a workable hypothesis. This view has been held by the majority of people in every age (even our own, outside the sphere of Western culture) and many of them have described experiences of that reality. Just because our own religious faith has broken down under the impact of positivism is no reason to put religion on the shelf. Instead, it is time to examine the dogmas of naturalistic thought which deny that such experiences are possible, and this is just what Carl Jung has done. It is for this reason that I suggest that Christian counselors and pastors can receive encouragement and direction from Dr. Jung. He has truly tackled the problem of meaning.

Carl Jung's Insight

Jung has made as great strides as anyone in our time in treating this loss of meaning; the twenty volumes of his collected works represent the results. Many of his patients were engineers and scientists who came to him because they had lost their sense of meaning. We cannot go into his point of view in detail in the space we have here (this I have done in Chapter 11 of *Healing and Christianity*, and again in *Encounter with God*). Jung is a careful and critical thinker whose conclusions about the present world-view are important. He criticizes the assumption that man is in a self-contained space-time box, touched only by the physical world, and shows that modern science has broken out of this model of the universe. There is thus no good reason to deny that a reality from outside the physical or psychological box can touch men and women. There actually is a reality in which one can have confidence and trust, a reality which provides meaning. It is just a matter of experiencing, seeing and understanding that reality.

Jung was consulted by people from all over the world. He summarized the importance of meaning to them in these words, which have been more widely quoted than anything else he wrote:

> Among all my patients in the second half of life—that is to say, over thirty-five—there has not been one whose problem in the last resort was not that of finding a religious outlook on life. It is safe to say that every one of them fell ill because he had lost that which the living religions of every age have given to their followers, and none of them has been really healed who did not regain his religious outlook.[5]

Much of the neurotic distress that I see among college students is the result of having lost religious faith. Their neurosis is often a religious experience in reverse. The traditional faith no longer speaks to these students, and no one offers them anything else. They often wish to talk with someone who is able to present them with a religious tradition that has meaning and reality for them. They sometimes wonder why so few have shown interest in their need. After World War II, Jung spoke to the similar problem of the troubled peoples of devastated Europe in these clear words:

Everything now depends on man: immense power of destruction is given into his hand, and the question is whether he can resist the will to use it, and can temper his will with the spirit of love and wisdom. He will hardly be capable of doing so on his own unaided resources. He needs the help of an "advocate" in heaven, that is, of the child who was caught up to God and who brings the "healing" and making whole of the hitherto fragmentary man.[6]

It is not only those who must avoid neurosis who need to find meaning. There are people everywhere who need the same meaning.

The Need Today

For fifteen years I directed a psychological clinic at St. Luke's Church in Monrovia, California, where again and again we were faced with problems of loss of meaning. Until we searched for ways of dealing with this problem, we were often unable to help those who were suffering. I do not find the situation appreciably different among the students at Notre Dame, or among the groups I meet lecturing throughout this country and abroad. Some people have deep roots of faith and are not threatened by the disbelief of our age. Others find meaning through the Pentecostal experience, the Jesus movement, or Cursillo. But there are many who are not and probably cannot be touched in any of these ways, and many of them seek solutions through counseling. Yet there are still relatively few religious counselors to whom these people can turn. The people in need are there, waiting for us. This is one of our tasks in life, to help:

Those who fear that they are alone, in the midst of a meaningless or hostile universe, who have never experienced a center of reality which has power and which cares. .

The men and women who are angry because they stand defenseless against a purely neutral or destructive society and world, who do not suspect that there is a loving concern in the universe which reaches out to those who are helped to see and seek it. . . .

The person who is chained to a lead weight of depression, who does not dream that such a life could be touched and changed by an experience of meaning and value. . . .

None of these experiences is easy to mediate but the importance and satisfaction of helping people find meaning which they have lost is greater than we can even guess. In addition, the counselors who are able to lead the way receive several extra dividends themselves.

Primarily, their own contact with the source of meaning and purpose is renewed, usually when this is most needed. They no longer have to rely on themselves alone, as the transforming agent. Thus the counselors come to see themselves more as re- movers of roadblocks than as healers who have ultimate respon- sibility. They find that they are only the catalyst, enabling the other persons to seek their own healing. Each of them becomes more free, then, to do his or her own part, and this brings growth for the counselor, as well as for the counselee.

In addition, one of the principal problems of the counseling situation becomes easier to resolve. This is transference, or the emotional dependence of the hurting person on the counselor, which is difficult to lift once it has begun. Where there are no gods to worship or to deal with, a man or woman is often picked to fill the role of God, particularly the understanding, non- judgmental counselor. But when the counselor and counselee both realize that the healing and transformation come from be- yond the counseling situation, then the transference/counter- transference situation is put into proper perspective. As it is resolved, each of them, enriched by a new human relationship, shares the meaning that is given to each and the reality each has found. Adolf Guggenbühl-Craig has written wisely of the dan- gers in helping people in his perceptive book *Power in the Helping Professions*.

If, as so many have asserted, there is such a reality which people can seek in relationship together, then it is important for the counselor to keep an eye peeled for problems of meaning. Usually only the trained counselor, after careful study, can determine whether the person's problem is an ordinary psychological one, or is from this deeper need. It may well be that problems of meaning require a specialty within the counseling profession. Religious experts who are competent to help with things of the soul are hard to find, and there is, of course, real difficulty about referring a person with whom a relationship has been established. For this reason, a counselor's counselor in these matters might offer a possible solution.

Where the problem is one of meaning and purpose, the principal task is to encourage the individual to search for the transpersonal reality which can fill one's need. There are first the records of those who speak of this reality; then the person can turn to his/her own experience. The counselor's own experience will play a part in the confidence and trust he/she imparts, but there are specific guidelines as to how the search can be directed. These have been described by many of the devotional masters, for instance by Baron von Hügel, as well as by Jung, and I have discussed them in *Encounter with God*.

In a sense, the person who intervenes with meaning is stepping into another person's universe in order to suggest ways of seeking meaning. One way is in helping the other person remove roadblocks to finding meaning. This may be the only way to help many people in the problems they have with themselves and others, and it may well offer the counselor values just as great. Next we shall ask how individuals can prepare themselves to intervene in this way with meaning.

Facilitating Meaning

There is a real problem relating to those who have lost their sense of meaning and purpose, who have been cut off from their religious roots. It does no good to say to them: "Now snap out of it! Have faith." This is exactly what they can*not* do. The person is no more able to have faith than the neurotic is able to snap out of a phobia or projection. In fact, trying to argue or preach the other person into faith usually only increases the person's guilt and tension. One who is caught like this is in much the same spot as Christian Scientists who believe that sickness is the result of error, and then find themselves suffering with cancer. They are sick and guilty at the same time.

Many Christians have a strange attitude toward disbelief and disbelievers. They treat them as the worst of sinners and shun them the way that many people shun the sick and the poor. Yet if there *is* a meaningful reality which we humans can know and be touched by, and we are unable to find it, the trouble is with our understanding and our experience; our morals are not defective. Perhaps the reason for this attitude toward agnostics and atheists is the unconscious lack of belief on the part of many Christians in the last three or four hundred years. Condemning others may well be the Christians' personal reaction to their own unconscious doubt. It threatens them to have to face and handle someone who does not believe as they say they do.

What can counselors do to prepare themselves to help the person who cannot believe and because of this is suffering a neurosis of meaning? Before anything else, of course, those who tackle problems of meaning must have the ability, the skills and training as any other counselor must. But they need other qualifications as well. I believe that there are four of them: *one*, they need to recognize doubt as a real problem; *two*, they will have developed an intellectual framework in which meaning has a place; *three*, they will know certain practices which lead toward meaning; and *four*, they will be themselves an example of the meaning to which they direct the person seeking meaning. Let us look at each of these qualifications.

The Wounded Healer

It is nearly impossible for a counselor to help the ones who have lost their faith in a meaningful universe unless the counselors themselves have wrestled with their own problems of meaning. The person who has never had any doubts is simply unable to comprehend what someone suffering an existential neurosis is enduring. In this situation there is almost nothing so annoying as a visit from another person who is full of joy and happiness and cannot understand what on earth is the matter with the gloomy friend. I remember once when I was going through some dark and difficult times, and I had an assistant who had just had a tremendous religious experience and was bubbling over with joy. He came to me quite concerned because he wondered what was the matter with my faith that I did not show more joy. It was bad enough to be enduring darkness without this kind of judgment on top of it.

The idea of the wounded healer (the one who is able to heal because he has suffered and come through illness) is perhaps more useful in dealing with loss of meaning than in any other area. One who has struggled through the problem can reach out a hand and offer a way. Experience and conviction are of course necessary. The counselor who has found no meaning, or who simply doubts that there is any, will obviously not be of much help. But belief without doubt behind it is truly questionable. Rigidity of belief is most often a defense mechanism to protect one from having to face one's own uncertainties, and doubt which remains unconscious only reinforces the doubts of those who are seeking help. The person sitting opposite to me often sees into my unconscious better than I do.

The wounded healers in this case, then, are those who have had the courage to look within and deal with their own inner doubts and uncertainties and find at least some answers. Or, if their doubts were less conscious, they may have penetrated into the unconscious depths to discover that doubt which is common to nearly all of us. Doubt is our human condition, and by wrestling with it, one finds that there is a way and a reality in which to believe, and there is also a confidence to give to another. Any other confidence rests on very shaky grounds. Adolf Guggenbühl-Craig's *Power in the Helping Professions*, to which I have already referred, gives an excellent introduction to the reality of the wounded healer.

An Intellectual Framework

While the counseling process relies largely on affective and emotional skills and disciplines, there is a place, particularly in relation to meaning, for intellectual or cognitive content. It is not a matter of either affective (emotional or feeling) skill *or* knowledge, but of both knowledge and affective skill. This is difficult for us human beings, who like to see things one side at a time. Yet if we were teaching organic chemistry or differential calculus today, we would not expect the students to discover it on their own. We expect them to be given direct knowledge and explanation. At the same time they will be more likely to learn with a warm affective climate to help the learning along. Similarly, in today's confused and troubled world, where some of the keenest minds have doubted, we are wise not to expect people to discover belief on their own. They need both content and a warm understanding climate as well.

When people state that there is *no* spirit, no God, no meaning, they are stating a denial that something exists and most denial systems are very dogmatic. From a logical point of view, a denial that something exists is the most difficult statement to support. Those who make such statements are saying either that they know *everything* about the world, or that they know the *essential reality* of the world. In other words, either they have *seen* that the "thing" does not exist, or they have *proved* that it is impossible. Either one assumes a lot more knowledge than most scientists are willing to grant. Human beings simply don't know enough about the world to deny much of anything categorically. And in much the same way, if one insists that the human being is completely contained in a physical, space-time world, one is inferring a denial statement about any reality beyond, and this denial cannot be supported.

There was a time when men and women thought they knew all about the world in which we live. In the late nineteenth century, people really believed that they were approaching complete explanation of human beings and the world, on the basis of the physical laws of Newton, the ninety-two atoms (like billiard balls), and the evolutionary principle of Darwin. Most psychologists and theologians are still caught back in that intellectual framework. As I have shown in some detail in my book, *Encounter with God*, the science of the twentieth century has robbed us of our optimistic belief that we have knowledge of all reality. One after another, the scientists such as Mme. Curie, Becquerel, Bohr, Heisenberg, and Einstein introduced new facts which showed how wrong the nineteenth-century scientists had been in thinking that human beings could arrive at final truths. Science itself has discarded the idea of certainty or of final truths. Instead it sees scientific knowledge only in terms of hypotheses (unproved theories that can be tentatively accepted to explain certain facts) which may well be overturned tomorrow and replaced. And, therefore, sophisticated science is careful to avoid telling what is *not* in the universe (which someone may discover tomorrow).

This attitude is easily grasped by people today and particularly by students. One paper turned in by a student for a class in "The Theological Foundations of Religious Instruction" is typical of the attitude of many students who are searching for meaning. He wrote that the religious classes in high school had done little to convince him of the reality of the spiritual world or of religion in general. His paper went on:

> I had received an excellent training in the sciences from grade school on, and I was operating on the assumption that science would inevitably discover everything that could be possibly known about reality. I was a positivist without knowing it.

Starting with this faith in materialistic science, he was then led by a physics teacher

> . . . through Heisenberg's uncertainty principle, and in doing so the ultimate mysteriousness of reality, even physical reality, was revealed to me. It is significant that the intellectual experience that was probably the one most important experience in allowing me to reconcile myself with my religion came not in a religious course, but in a physics course.

What was true of this student will also be true of the counselee caught in the nihilism and skepticism of the nineteenth century. Can the counselor deal with it? For this student, it took only a little training in modern science to open a new perspective.

The discoveries of Freud pointed toward the reality of the psyche and psychic causation, and this opened the door to twentieth-century psychotherapy and counseling. In the 1930's the discoveries of Dr. Flanders Dunbar and other researchers in psychosomatic medicine revealed that the physical body is not just a mechanical system. Instead it works in intimate relation with emotional states. At the same time Carl Jung was coming to the conclusion that destructive emotional states can be healed only as one is brought into contact with a transpersonal reality. As meaning is given by this reality, the fear and anger and depression are often transmuted. Finally, the anthropological studies of Teilhard de Chardin and Loren Eiseley have shown that the simplistic system of Darwin is not adequate to deal with the fact of human development. It therefore seems necessary to assume that there is a purpose other than the human ego operating through reality and drawing us toward some meaningful goal.

If all this is true, then our picture of humankind and the world is much more complex than we once thought. The model of the nineteenth-century physicists and the twentieth-century behaviorists is no longer adequate to describe the human being. We can no longer say that the human being is only consciousness operating in a completely knowable space-time world. This model accounts for only part of the facts, and those who maintain it have to deny certain data in order to do so; and that is not good science. When the recent developments in psychology, physical science, evolution, and psychical research are taken into account, we are forced to present a complex picture of mankind and reality—the diagram which we have presented before and now present again for convenience sketches human consciousness. We have a deep and hidden part of our personality which is called the "assumptive world" by Jerome Frank, and *the unconscious* by Freud and Jung.

The human being has great depth, and, even more important, it is through this unfathomed unconscious part that we obtain insights and intuitions which give us an understanding of

A Model or Scheme

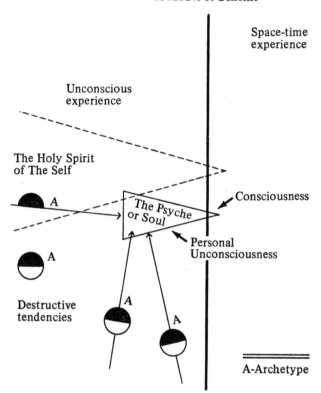

even the physical world. Through the unconscious we also receive experiences of a non-space-time world, a realm which appears to be even more diverse and complex than the one of sense experience. Within this world there is no question that one discovers destructive realities as well as positive ones. Mythology speaks of the monsters which guard the entrance of the other world, and folklore has described them well.

But here one also finds the source of creative power and strength, of concern which seems to seek humans out and succor them, and which alone can sustain and rescue them from the powers of darkness and destruction. The counselor's task when someone has lost meaning is to facilitate or make easier the individual's openness to this creative aspect of reality, and to give guidance so that the person can avoid those dark parts of the unconscious which cannot be assimilated. This requires wisdom *and* discernment, both of this individual's stage of life and growth and also of spiritual reality itself.

How?

The next question is: How can this point of view be made easier or facilitated in experience? And how can it be verified or confirmed in experience? It is difficult to explain a whole way of life in a few pages, but let me try. To start with, it is important to realize that we Westerners are as underdeveloped in our understanding and differentiation of our inner life as Eastern people are in their understanding of the outer physical world.

Once people believe that they contain something beyond consciousness, then they can take the time to be still and look within. Human beings can seldom discover much about the inner world until they do take the time to be silent, and quiet, and look within. They are often amazed by what they discover about themselves and the psyche.

Dreams have been called the royal road to understanding this inner being. From earliest times the dream has been viewed as giving entrance to another dimension of reality. Dreams were once seen as the way through which God and spiritual powers spoke to man. As human beings recover from the brainwashing of dogmatic, materialistic science, they see more and more evidence in their dream life of unknown things. Dreams reveal not only forgotten parts of themselves but also inherited and undiscovered parts within the psyche. They even give an entrance to a spiritual reality which surrounds human beings.

Through dreams they not only can find the destructive aspect of reality, but they can experience and come into the presence of the very numinous, creative, caring part of reality as well. Learning to interpret a dream is like learning a foreign language. But there is no easy Berlitz system, and no dream dictionary will help. One has to watch for connections, and also look for various symbols and what they mean. The symbols in a dream often can have meaning for people, and if we want to become catalysts for other people we must know all that we can about myths and symbols. After studying these elements, we then must wait until the particular meaning of the dream just comes to us or emerges. I have found that it impressed agnostic students when they were asked to watch their dreams carefully and write them down over a period of time. Some meaning from beyond the student's ego appears to be working within them, and once they experience this, their disbelief begins to crumble. They experience that there is something that is wiser than themselves that is guiding them.

Another way of tapping this area is through developing one's ability to use fantasy and imagination. The same depths of the unconscious can be tapped and made conscious through writing or painting, through yoga, the dance, or modeling in clay. In these ways we can learn to look within and begin to see some of our bubbling inner life, and let our own conscious mind direct the process. This method is similar to the Christian practice of meditation. As I have shown in the last chapter, it can be used to know and relate to the spiritual forces, the angels and demons that influence us and become parts of the human soul. This is discernment in action.

Jung has called this practice active imagination, in which moods and emotions are allowed to be changed into images so that one is able to begin to deal with them. There are almost unlimited uses for fantasy and imagination in counseling, especially in counseling those with a problem of meaning. An understanding of the dream and the imagination are very helpful in developing discernment.

A record of one's going into and meeting or encountering this inner world is important and so one should keep a journal or spiritual log. One should record one's intuitions, one's dreams and interpretations of them, sometimes poetry or stories, and one's imaginings and reactions to both inner and outer events. Few experiences are more convincing than reviewing a record of this kind. We realize that we are not as simple as some people would like us to believe. By looking back over one's own experiences, one can see that we may well be in touch with another realm of reality which is different from that of the senses and the physical world.

Any one of these suggestions could be expanded into a full

book, and yet this would not tell the story. To experience the depth within, and in this way to discover the depth of another level of reality, takes time and effort. One has to learn the way by trying oneself. The church once knew how to approach this other reality. But the church has been so taken in by the materialism of the nineteenth-century science that it not only rejected its own practice, but then forgot that humankind had any need to deal with the realm of the spirit. It is clear that one often has to start all over again, often without the church's guidance, and counselors have to try out and know the experiences themselves before they can guide others. As with any matter of experience, *one can lead another no further than one has been oneself.*

Example

There is one more requirement for anyone who is trying to lead other persons who have lost their sense of meaning back to meaning. This is probably the most demanding and difficult part of the process. There is no way for a counselor to convince another person that any source of creative power and concern actually exists unless one can show its effect on oneself. How does anyone realize that there is a loving God? Usually the first realization is given to the child through loving parents. And as we learn painfully in society, the child who is not given this love grows up severely crippled, and sometimes criminal.

One can speak words forever about loving concern in the universe, but they will not be taken seriously by individuals who have lost their faith until they experience loving actions toward themselves. There are counselees who sometimes deliberately try to test counselors. They refuse to take the counselor seriously until they see whether they can turn the counselor against them or whether the counselor will still show loving action toward them no matter what they do. Often a person's change begins once the counselor has passed such a test.

I was once on both the giving and receiving ends in this way. It was a time when one of my children was having difficulty in school, and I found myself sitting opposite a psychologist. He informed me that this child's main problem was that he did not believe that I really cared for him. I complained that when I tried to show interest and concern, it was rejected. And the psychologist came back: "Has it ever occurred to you that he is testing you to see just how much you do care?" I took him seriously and managed to show this child that I did care. The results were dramatic. How can one expect adults, with their full-grown suspicions, to be any less demanding than our children?

James Hillman has spoken about the difficulty of dealing with depressed and suicidal patients in his sensitive little book *Suicide and the Soul.* Speaking of the potential suicide (and one must remember that this person has simply reached the logical conclusion of depression and meaninglessness), Hillman reminds counselors that in this situation their inner attitude will be found out. Often the counselor gets so fed up and bored trying to be with and help the suicidal counselee that unconsciously he would like to have the patient stop bothering him. When this happens often suicide does take place. We had better know our inner selves before the counselees discover what we are like. We can then submit to the rigorous training it takes to show care and concern for the person who is suffering real depression.

Most people who have enough problems to look for real help have at least some need for this kind of meaning. Somewhere along the line, they have been denied the effects of positive affection, of love. And this final ingredient is the most important one the counselor can add to the pot. In part it comes from conscious effort, and in part it is inseparable from one's own being. And perhaps this is the reason one becomes and goes on working as a counselor. When counselors try to provide this ingredient, they are forced to reconcile the various parts of themselves and care about counselees no matter what. The counselor at the same time must give the counselee the security of knowing he/she can act like a spoiled brat and still be cared for. Of course, the counselor will also never let the relationship become one which is harmful to the counselee, morally or spiritually.

One may well ask: What is the difference between this kind of counseling and religious education? And the answer is that there is little difference, except that in religious education one is trying to answer the questions before they have been asked. In the counseling situation, people are asking why they hurt, or why they cause concern to those around them. For those whose problem is essentially that of loss of meaning, the answers come most effectively from a counselor who has wrestled with the problem of doubt; who can provide meaning through a solid intellectual framework; who can open a door to meaning through inward turning and meditation, through the dream and imagination; and finally who is trying to manifest the reality of loving concern, of which we all speak, sometimes loosely.

There is probably no illness more pervasive in the Western world than loss of meaning, and no task which challenges the religious counselor more. In our time men and women are needed who are trained to deal with this problem of love and faith, with wisdom and discernment. Such people can lead people through evil to meaning and through ecstasy without superstition and stupidity.

Notes

Chapter I

1. Andrew M. Greeley, *The Sociology of the Paranormal—A Reconnaissance.* Sage Publications, Inc., Beverly Hills, Cal. 1975. The same material was presented by Greeley and an associate in an article for the *New York Times Magazine*, Jan. 27, 1975. This study has been recently replicated in Great Britain by two researchers, David Hay and Ann Morisy of Manchester College, Oxford and the University of Nottingham.

2. Simon and Schuster, New York, N.Y. 1977.

Chapter II

1. *Theological and Pastoral Orientations of the Catholic Charismatic Renewal.* Malines, Belgium, 1974. This paper is printed in the United States by Ave Maria Press, Notre Dame, Indiana.

2. These books are *The Christian and the Supernatural* (Minneapolis, Augsburg Publishing House, 1976), *God, Dreams, and Revelation* (Minneapolis, Augsburg Publishing House, 1974), *Healing and Christianity* (New York, Harper & Row, 1973), and *Tongue Speaking* (Garden City, New York, Doubleday & Company, Inc., 1964).

3. The Rev. George A. Maloney, S.J., has dealt wisely with psychic experiences like these in his paper "How To Understand and Evaluate the Charismatics' Newest Experience: 'Slaying in the Spirit'," in *Crux of the News*, Crux Extra, November 1, 1976.

4. *Ibid.*, p. 1.

5. David St. Clair, *Psychic Healers.* Garden City, New York, Doubleday & Company, Inc., 1974, p. 312.

6. George Maloney, *op. cit.*, p. 2.

7. *Loc. cit.*

8. *Ibid.*, p. 1. One friend, however, has told me of a mishap that paid dividends. In falling she did not "float" but went down somewhat heavily, knocking off and breaking the glasses of a man next to her. When she rose and realized what had happened, she picked up the glasses and waited for the man. She asked him to stay nearby while she went out and had them fixed. But he was nowhere in sight when she returned. She had to hunt for him; it was then she learned that he was a lonely and destitute alcoholic who had dropped in for the service as a last resort. One of the team had spotted him sitting alone and asked him to come and hear a talk about the experience they had just had. A conversion experience had just taken place, and as a direct result of the acci-

dent, the man was quickly rehabilitated. For several years he has been working full time for the center where the incident happened.

9. Mircea Eliade, *Shamanism: Archaic Techniques of Ecstasy.* Princeton, New Jersey, Princeton University Press, 1964, pp. 4 and 5.

10. Eusebius, *Ecclesiastical History,* 16.

11. Ronald A. Knox, *Enthusiasm: A Chapter in the History of Religion.* Oxford, The Clarendon Press, 1950, p. 124.

12. Maloney, *op. cit.,* p. 1.

13. Andrew Canale, *Masters of the Heart: Science, Religion and the Spiritual Quest.* New York: Paulist Press, 1978.

Chapter III

1. *God Dreams in Revelation.* Augsburg Press, Minneapolis, Minnesota, 1974, Chapter 4.

2. Victor White, O.P., *God and the Unconscious.* The World Publishing Co., Cleveland, 1961, p. 203.

3. *Ibid.,* pp. 192f.

4. This list of biblical references and those following are reproduced in similar form in my book, *Tongue Speaking: An Experiment in Spiritual Experience.* Doubleday & Co., Inc., Garden City, New York, 1964, Appendix A.

Aggelos—angel, as messenger or agent:

MATTHEW	MARK	LUKE	JOHN	ACTS
1:20,24	1:13	1:11,13,18,	1:51	5:19
2:13,19	8:38	19,26,28,	5:4	6:15
4:6,11	12:25	30,34,35,	12:29	7:30,35,38,
13:39,41,49	13:27,32	38	20:12	53
16:27		2:9,10,13		8:26
18:10		15,21		10:3,7,22
22:30		4:10		11:13
24:31,36		7:27		12:7,8,9,10
25:31,41		9:26		11,15,23
26:53		12:8,9		23:8,9
28:2,5		15:10		27:23
		16:22		
		20:36*		
		22:43		
		24:23		

*Isaggelos—equal to or like the angels.

5. Excerpts from a letter written by Mrs. Wortley, wife of the Rev. Canon E. J. Wortley of Jamaica, British West Indies, to her daughter, September 18, 1928:

. . . Your dad had a wonderful death-bed. He was ill exactly ten weeks; at first he had a slight stroke, as I told you. . . . On the Friday before he died he was in one of his sweetest moods, quite clear in his mind. We were having our usual talk, and he was praying that his sufferings would soon be over; we talked of the people he hoped to see, and I reminded him of Archbishop Nuttall and one or two of our East Indian friends who had died. And he said, "Oh! joy unspeakable! I had not thought of seeing them in Paradise."

Then later, he suddenly said to me, "Aunt Janie has come with the Angels." And after a few moments he said it again in the calmest, most natural way. Then he stretched his arm across the bed and seemed to shake hands all up the side of the bed; so I said, "What are you doing?" to which he said, "Shaking hands with the Angels." Then he turned to me as I stood next to him, and touching me gently he said, "Just move a little, you are blocking the way of one of the Angels." And in a most reproving voice, he said, "You may not know the Angels, but I know them all."

. . . Later on that day, he said, "Oh! my, and do I have to have another night of torment . . .?" So I said, "Of course not, how could you? When the Angels have come . . .?" But he said quietly, "They have gone." I told him, "Oh! never mind; so long as they have been here, you may be sure they came to clear the atmosphere and put a stop to all the Devil's work, and you will have no more suffering." Well, he had a good night, and next day he continued comfortable. At mid-day on Saturday he began again to talk with the Angels.

He said, "Angels, Angels, are you the same Angels who came before?" Twice over he said it, and then "Two Arch-Angels. . . . Two Arch-Angels. . . ." And he went on talking, beginning every sentence, "The Angels . . ." but finishing in such an indistinct voice that we could not hear what he said, until we heard, "Angels, Angels, ready? ready?" And he settled himself, lying flat on his back with his arms up in such a way, trying to ease up, that you could imagine you saw the Angels bending over him to take him up. . . .

And the letter goes on to tell of his lying peacefully until he died, finally in a coma. One of the other stories mentioned is quite similar in feeling. The third tells of being wakened before dawn to a vision of two shining beings who stood waiting beside a window; as she watched, puzzled, the woman saw her mother appear, and together the three persons glided by the bed, close enough to touch, and disappeared, leaving the room electrified and glowing with light. The woman lay rejoicing that her mother, who had been sick, was now so well and filled with health. At that moment she heard the telephone, and listened to her husband take the message that her mother had died a few moments before.

6. Pneuma akatharton—unclean spirit:

MATTHEW	MARK	LUKE	ACTS
10:1	1:23,26,27	4:36	5:16
12:43	3:11,30	6:18	8:7
	5:2,8,13	8:29	
	6:7	9:39,42	
	7:25	11:24	
	9:25		

7. *Pneuma*—spirit, in various senses: Spirit, apparition, spirit of an unclean demon, of those possessed by demons, evil spirit, spirit causing infirmity, deaf and dumb spirit, python spirit, spirit of divination:

MATTHEW	MARK	LUKE	ACTS
8:16	6:49	4:33	16:16,18
12:45	9:17,20,25	7:21	19:12,13,15,
14:26		8:2	16
		10:20	23:8,9
		11:26	
		13:11	
		24:37,39	

8. The Athenians felt that Paul had a strange demon to set forth, but they listened, and some of them became followers (Acts 17:18). The Jews considered that John the Baptist was abstemious because he had a demon (Mt. 11:18; Lk. 7:33), and that Jesus must have a demon to preach such strange things (Jn. 8:48, 52; 10:20). Certainly some of us might wish to have a "demon" like one of these, but we had better take a second look at who it was that was so "possessed."

9. Joseph Henry Thayer, *Greek-English Lexicon of the New Testament*, American Book Company, New York, 1889, p. 123.

10. Daimonizomai—to be demonized, possessed by a devil:

MATTHEW	MARK	LUKE	JOHN
4:24	1:32	8:36	10:21
8:16,28,33	5:15,16,18		
9:32			
12:22			
15:22			

11. *Daimon, daimonion*—god, inferior divinity, demon, shade, defied spirit:

MATTHEW	MARK	LUKE	JOHN	ACTS
7:22	1:34,39	4:33,35,41	7:20	17:18
8:31	3:15,22	7:33	8:48,49,52	
9:33,34	5:12	8:2,27,29,	10:20,21	
10:8	6:13	30,33,35		
11:18	7:26,29,30	38		
12:24,27,28	9:38	9:1,42,49		
17:18	16:9,17	10:17		
		11:14,15,18,		
		19,20		
		13:32		

12. Thayer, *op. cit.*, p. 135.

13. *Satan, diabolos, Beelzeboul*—adversary, calumniator, false accuser, prince of demons, author of evil:

MATTHEW	MARK	LUKE	JOHN	ACTS
4:1,5,8,	1:13	4:2,3,5,	8:44	5:3
10,11	3:22,23,26	6,8,13	13:2,27	10:38
10:25	4:15	8:12		13:10
12:24,26,27		10:18		26:18
13:39		11:15,18,19		
25:41		13:16		
		22:3,31		

Archon (with *daimonion* or *kosmos*)—Prince of evil spirits, of this world:

MATTHEW	MARK	LUKE	JOHN
9:34	3:22	11:15	12:31
12:24			14:30
			16:11

Poneros or *ponerou*—evil, the evil one, the devil:

MATTHEW	LUKE	JOHN
5:37	11:4 (RL)	17:15
6:13		
13:19,38		

14. The following references in the epistles include angels, archangels, spirits, elemental, weak and beggarly spirits, spirits of slavery, of stupor, of error, demons, idols, gods, lords, thrones, dominions, principalities, powers, deceitful wiles, rulers, authorities, deceivers, elements that will be dissolved by fire, our weakness or infirmities, creatures of instinct, servants, flames of fire, Balaam's error, the devil (*archon*, *satan*, *poneros*), sin and death, power of death, master and servant, god of this age, evil age, prince of the power of the air, dominion of darkness, god working error, error, deceit, guile, error of lawless men, corruption in the world, anti-Christ:

Romans 5:12 ff.; 6:9 ff.; 7:23 ff.; 8:2,10,15,38; 11:8; 13:2.
1 Corinthians 2:6,12; 4:5; 5:5; 6:3; 7:5; 8:4 f., 7; 10:7,9 f., 19 ff.; 11:10; 12:2,10; 13:1; 15:24 ff.
2 Corinthians 1:10; 2:11; 4:4; 6:16; 7:10; 11:4,14; 12:7.
Galatians 1:4,8; 3:19; 4:3,8,9,14.
Ephesians 1:21; 2:2; 3:10; 4:27; 5:5; 6:11 f., 16.
Colossians 1:13,16; 2:8,10,15,18,20; 3:5.
1 Thessalonians 1:9; 2:3,18; 5:4 f.
2 Thessalonians 1:7; 2:3 f., 8 f., 11; 3:3.
1 Timothy 1:20; 3:6,7,16; 4:1; 5:15,21.
2 Timothy 1:7; 2:26.
Hebrews 1:4 ff.,13 f., 2:2,5,7,9,14 ff.; 3:13; 5:2; 6:8; 9:26; 12:1,4,9,22; 13:2.
James 2:19; 3:15; 4:7.
1 Peter 1:12; 3:19,22; 4:3; 5:8.
2 Peter 1:4; 2:4,11,12,18; 3:10,12,17.
1 John 2:13,14; 3:8,10,12; 4:1,3,6; 5:18,19,21.
2 John 7.
Jude 6,9,11,14.

15. Alexander Roberts and James Donaldson, eds., *The Ante-Nicene Fathers*. Wm. B. Eerdmans Publishing Co., Grand Rapids, Michigan, various dates:

Origen, Vol. 4, pp. 240f, 256f., 264ff.
Clement, Vol. 7, pp. 108ff.
Shepherd of Hermas, Vol. 2, p. 24.
Barnabas, Vol. 1, p. 148.
Ignatius, Vol. 1, pp. 68, 118.

16. *Ibid.*:
Justin Martyr, Vol. 1, p. 190.
Methodius, Vol. 7, p. 370.
Lactantius, Vol. 7, pp. 64ff., 232.

17. Philip Schaff, ed., *The Nicene and Post-Nicene Fathers*, First Series. Wm. B. Eerdmans Publishing Co., Grand Rapids, Michigan, 1956, Vol. II, *The City of God*, p. 511. In the same work Augustine discusses angels and demons at great length, particularly in Books VIII to XII, pp. 153ff., as well as in other works.

18. Gustaf Aulén, *Christus Victor: An Historical Study of the Three Main Types of the Idea of the Atonement*. The Macmillan Co., New York, 1951.

19. White, *op. cit.*, Chapters VI, VII and X. The discussion of Aquinas that follows is drawn largely from this work.

20. C. G. Jung, *Psychological Types*. Routledge & Kegan Paul Ltd., London, 1923, Glossary.

21. White, *op. cit.*, pp. 202f.

22. *The Great Ideas: A Syntopicon of the Great Books of the Western World*, Mortimer J. Adler, ed. Encyclopaedia Britannica, Inc., Chicago, 1952, Vol. I, Article on Angels, pp. 1ff.

23. James Kirsch, *Shakespeare's Royal Self*. G. P. Putnam's Sons, New York, 1966.

24. C. G. Jung, *Psychology and Religion: West and East*. Pantheon Books, New York, 1958, p. 289.

25. *Ibid.*, p. 486

26. *Ibid.*, p. 320

27. C. G. Jung, *Civilization in Transition*. Pantheon Books, New York, 1964, p. 212.

28. *C. G. Jung Letters, 2:1951-61*, ed. Gerhard Adler and Amila Jaffé. Princeton University Press, Princeton, New Jersey, 1975, p. 624.

29. Jung has presented a very clear picture of this kind of experience in Chapter VI of his autobiography, *Memories, Dreams, Reflections*. Pantheon Books, New York, 1963.

30. *The Book of Common Prayer* (proposed), according to the use of The Episcopal Church. New York: The Church Hymnal Corporation and The Seabury Press, 1977, p. 302.

Chapter IV

1. C. G. Jung, *Collected Works*, Vol. 9, Part II. *Aion: Researches into the Phenomenology of the Self*. New York: Pantheon Books, 1959, p. 70.

Chapter V

1. I have discussed Christian education in my book, *Can Christians Be Educated?* Religious Education Press, Mishawaka, Ind., 1977.

Chapter VI

1. U.S. Department of H.E.W., Office of the Assistant Secretary for Health and Scientific Affairs, "First Special Report to the U.S. Congress on Alcohol and Health," Health Services and Mental Health Administration/ National Institute of Mental Health/National Institute on Alcohol Abuse and Alcoholism, December, 1971.

2. *New York Times,* July 9, 1972, cover story, Section D.

3. Jerome D. Frank, *Persuasion and Healing.* 1st ed. New York, Schocken Books, 1963, pp. 233 f, and 66.

4. Alan McGlashan, *Gravity and Levity.* Boston, Houghton Mifflin Company, 1976, p. 37.

5. C. G. Jung, *Modern Man in Search of a Soul,* New York, Harcourt, Brace and Company, 1933, p. 229.

6. C. G. Jung, Collected Works, Vol. 11, *Psychology and Religion: West and East. Op. cit.,* p. 459.

Bibliography

Adler, Gerhard, *The Living Symbol*. Princeton, New Jersey: Princeton University Press, 1961.

The Ante-Nicene Fathers. Grand Rapids, Michigan: Wm. B. Eerdmans Publishing Co., various dates.

Aquinas, Saint Thomas, *The "Summa Theologica."* Literally translated by the Fathers of the English Dominican Province. London: Burns, Oates & Washbourne, various dates.

Aulén, Gustav, *Christus Victor: An Historical Study of the Three Main Types of the Idea of the Atonement*. New York: The Macmillan Co., 1951.

Berdyaev, Nicolas, *Dream and Reality: An Essay in Autobiography*. London: Geoffrey Bless, 1950.

Blatty, William P., *The Exorcist*. New York: Harper & Row, 1971.

The Book of Common Prayer (Proposed). According to the use of The Episcopal Church. New York: The Church Hymnal Corporation and The Seabury Press, 1977.

Bornkamm, Günther, *Jesus of Nazareth*. New York: Harper & Row, 1960.

Bristol, Claude, *The Magic of Believing*. Englewood Cliffs, New Jersey: Prentice-Hall, Inc., 1957.

Burrell, David B., *Exercises in Religious Understanding*. Notre Dame, Indiana: University of Notre Dame Press, 1975.

Campbell, Joseph, *The Hero with a Thousand Faces*. New York: Meridian Books, 1956.

―――, *Myths To Live By*. New York: Bantam Books, 1973.

Canale, Andrew, *Masters of the Heart*. New York: Paulist Press, 1978.

Castaneda, Carlos, *Journey to Ixtlan: The Lessons of Don Juan*. New York: Pocket Books, 1974.

―――, *A Separate Reality: Further Conversations with Don Juan*. New York: Simon and Schuster, 1971.

―――, *Tales of Power*. New York: Simon and Schuster, 1974.

―――, *The Teachings of Don Juan: A Yaqui Way of Knowledge*. Berkeley: University of California Press, 1968.

Christiani, Leon, *Evidences of Satan in the Modern World*. New York: The Macmillan Company, 1962.

Cox, Harvey, *Turning East: The Promise and Peril of the New Orientalism.* New York: Simon and Schuster, Inc., 1977.

De Zoete, Beryl, and Walter Spies, *Dance and Drama in Bali.* New York: Oxford University Press, 1974.

Dodds, E. R., *The Greeks and the Irrational.* Boston: Beacon Press, 1957.

Dunbar, Flanders, *Emotions and Bodily Changes.* 4th edition. New York: Columbia University Press, 1954.

Eiseley, Loren, *The Immense Journey.* New York: Random House, Inc., 1957.

Eliade, Mircea, *Shamanism: Archaic Techniques of Ecstasy.* Princeton, New Jersey: Princeton University Press, 1970.

Eliot, T. S., *The Complete Poems and Plays, 1909-1950.* New York: Harcourt, Brace & World, Inc., 1952.

Erikson, Erik H., *Childhood and Society.* New York: W. W. Norton & Co., Inc., 1964.

———, *Young Man Luther.* New York: W. W. Norton & Company, Inc., 1958.

Fordham, Michael, *Children as Individuals.* New York: G. P. Putnam's Sons, 1970.

Frank, Jerome D., *Persuasion and Healing.* 1st edition. New York: Schocken Books, 1969.

Freud, Sigmund, *The Future of an Illusion.* New York: Doubleday & Company, 1957.

———, *A General Introduction to Psychoanalysis.* New York: Washington Square Press, Inc., 1960.

Fuller, John G., *Arigo: Surgeon of the Rusty Knife.* New York: Thomas Y. Crowell Co., 1974.

The Great Ideas: A Syntopicon of Great Books of the Western World, Edited by Mortimer J. Adler. Chicago: Encyclopaedia Britannica, Inc., 1952. (Vol. I, Chapter 1: Angel)

Greeley, Andrew M., *Ecstasy: A Way of Knowing.* Englewood Cliffs, New Jersey: Prentice-Hall, Inc., 1974.

———, *The Sociology of the Paranormal: A Reconnaissance.* Beverly Hills, California: Sage Publications, Inc., 1975.

Guggenbühl-Craig, Adolf, *Power in the Helping Professions.* New York: Spring Publications, 1971.

Harper, Michael, *Spiritual Warfare.* Plainfield, New Jersey: Logos International, 1970.

Hagin, Kenneth, *Why Do People Fall under the Power?* (Tape). Tulsa, Oklahoma: Faith.

Hesse, Hermann, *Beneath the Wheel.* New York: Farrar, Straus and Giroux, 1968.

———, *Demian*. New York: Harper & Row, 1965.

———, *The Glass Bead Game: Magister Ludi*. New York: Holt, Rinehart & Winston, Inc., 1969.

———, *Narcissus and Goldmund*. New York: Farrar, Straus and Giroux, 1968.

———, *Steppenwolf*. New York: Holt, Rinehart & Winston, Inc., 1963.

Hillman, James, *Insearch: Psychology and Religion*. New York: Charles Scribner's Sons, 1968.

———, *Suicide and the Soul*. New York: Harper & Row, 1965

Hogg, James, *The Private Memoirs and Confessions of a Justified Sinner* New York: Grove Press, Inc., 1959.

Jacobi, Jolande, *Complex/Archetype/Symbol in the Psychology of C. G. Jung*. London: Routledge & Kegan Paul, 1959.

Joad, Cyril E., *The Recovery of Belief*. New York: The Macmillan Company, 1953.

Johnson, Robert A., *He!* New York: Harper & Row, 1977.

———, *She!* New York: Harper & Row, 1977.

C. G. Jung, *Analytical Psychology: Its Theory and Practice*. The Tavistock Lectures. New York: Random House, 1968.

———, *Collected Works*. Princeton, New Jersey: Princeton University Press for the Bollingen Foundation: Vol. 6, *Psychological Types*, 1971.

———, *Collected Works*. New York: Pantheon Books for the Bollingen Foundation:

Vol. 8, *The Structure and Dynamics of the Psyche*, 1960.

Vol. 9, Part II, *Aion: Researches into the Phenomenology of the Self*, 1959.

Vol. 10, *Civilization in Transition*, 1964.

Vol. 11, *Psychology and Religion: West and East*, 1958.

Vol. 15, *The Spirit in Man, Art, and Literature*, 1966.

Vol. 17, *The Development of Personality*, 1954.

———, *Memories, Dreams, Reflections*. Recorded and edited by Aniela Jaffé. New York: Random House, 1963.

———, *Modern Man in Search of a Soul*. New York: Harcourt, Brace and Company, 1933.

Jung, Carl G., *et al.*, *Man and His Symbols*. Garden City, New York: Doubleday & Company, Inc., 1964.

Kelsey, Morton (T.), *Can Christians Be Educated?* Mishawaka, Indiana: Religious Education Press, Inc., 1977.

———, *The Christian and the Supernatural*. Minneapolis: Augsburg Publishing House, 1976.

———, "Confronting Inner Violence." *The Journal of Pastoral Counseling* 7, no. 1 (January 1968): 61-78.

————, *Encounter with God: A Theology of Christian Experience.* Minneapolis: Bethany Fellowship, Inc., 1972. Also *Study Guide: Encounter with God*, 1975.

————, "Facing Death and Suffering: A Group Experiment in Affective Learning." *Lumen Vitae* (Brussels) 28 (1973), no. 2: 281-295.

————, *God, Dreams, and Revelation.* Minneapolis: Augsburg Publishing House, 1974.

————, *Healing and Christianity.* New York: Harper & Row, 1973.

————, *Myth, History and Faith.* New York: Paulist Press, 1974.

————, *The Other Side of Silence: A Guide to Christian Meditation.* New York: Paulist Press, 1976.

————, "Rediscovering the Priesthood through the Unconscious." *Journal of Pastoral Counseling* 7, no. 1 (Spring-Summer 1972): 26-36.

————, *Tongue Speaking: An Experiment in Spiritual Experience.* Garden City, New York: Doubleday & Company, Inc., 1964.

Kirsch, James, *Shakespeare's Royal Self.* New York: G. P. Putnam's Sons, 1966.

Kluger, Rivkah Schärf, *Satan in the Old Testament.* Evanston, Illinois: Northwestern University Press, 1967.

Knox, Ronald A., *Enthusiasm: A Chapter in the History of Religion.* Oxford: The Clarendon Press, 1950.

Kohlberg, Lawrence, "Education, Moral Development and Faith." *Journal of Moral Education* IV (October 1974).

Kohlberg, Lawrence, and Elliot Turiel, "Moral Development and Moral Education," in G. Lesser, ed., *Psychology and Educational Practice.* Chicago: Scott, Foresman and Co., 1971.

Kübler-Ross, Elisabeth, *On Death and Dying.* New York, Macmillan Publishing Co., Inc., 1969.

Kuhlman, Kathryn, *I Believe in Miracles.* Englewood Cliffs, New Jersey: Prentice-Hall, Inc., 1962.

————, *God Can Do It Again.* Englewood Cliffs, New Jersey: Prentice-Hall, Inc., 1969.

Kuhn, Thomas S., *The Structure of Scientific Revolutions.* 2nd edition. Chicago, The University of Chicago Press, 1970.

Lamb, F. Bruce, *The Wizard of the Upper Amazon.* Boston: Houghton Mifflin Co., 1975.

Lame Deer and Erdoes, Richard, *Lame Deer: Seeker of Visions.* New York: Simon and Schuster, 1972.

Lewis, C. S., *The Chronicles of Narnia (The Lion, the Witch and the Wardrobe, Prince Caspian, The Voyage of the Dawn Treader, The Silver Chair, The Horse and His Boy, The Magician's Nephew, The Last Battle).* New York: Macmillan Publishing Co., Inc., 1970.

——, *The Great Divorce*. New York: The Macmillan Company, 1957.

——, *The Screwtape Letters*. New York: The Macmillan Company, 1952.

——, *Space Trilogy (Out of the Silent Planet, Perelandra, That Hideous Strength)*. New York: Macmillan Publishing Co., Inc., 1965.

Lovejoy, Arthur O., *The Revolt Against Dualism*. New York: W. W. Norton & Company, Inc., 1930.

Lynch, James J., *The Broken Heart*. New York: Basic Books, Inc., 1977.

Luke, Helen M., *Dark Wood to White Rose: A Study of Meanings in Dante's Divine Comedy*. Pecos, New Mexico: Dove Publications, 1975.

MacNutt, Francis, O.P., *The Power To Heal*. Notre Dame, Indiana: Ave Maria Press, 1977.

MacDonald, George, *Phantastes and Lilith*. London: Victor Gollancz Ltd., 1962.

Mahoney, Maria F., *The Meaning in Dreams and Dreaming: The Jungian Viewpoint*. New York: The Citadel Press, 1970.

Maloney, George A., S.J., "How To Understand and Evaluate the Charismatics' Newest Experience: 'Slaying in the Spirit'." *Crux of the News*, Crux Extra, November 1, 1976.

McGlashan, Alan, *Gravity and Levity*. Boston: Houghton Mifflin Co., 1976.

——, *The Savage and the Beautiful Country*. New York: Stonehill Publishing Co., Inc., 1976.

Menninger, Karl A., *Man Against Himself*. New York: Harcourt, Brace and Company, 1938.

Moody, Raymond A., Jr., *Life After Life*. New York: Bantam Books, 1976.

——, *Reflections on Life After Life*. New York: Bantam Books, 1977.

Myers, Isabel Briggs, *Introduction to Type*. Privately printed (321 Dickinson Avenue, Swarthmore, Pennsylvania 19081), 1970.

Neihardt, John G., *Black Elk Speaks: Being the Life Story of a Holy Man of the Oglala Sioux*. Lincoln, Nebraska, University of Nebraska Press, 1961.

Neumann, Erich, *The Origins and History of Consciousness*. New York: Pantheon Books, 1954.

Newcomb, Franc Johnson, *Hosteen Klah: Navaho Medicine Man and Sand Painter*. Norman, Oklahoma: University of Oklahoma Press, 1964.

Oppenheimer, Robert, "Analogy in Science." *The American Psychologist* 11 (1956): 127-135.

Osis, Karlis, *Deathbed Observations by Physicians and Nurses*. (Monograph). New York: Parapsychology Foundation, 1961.

Perrin, Norman, *Rediscovering the Teaching of Jesus.* New York: Harper & Row, 1967.

Reich, Charles A., *The Greening of America.* New York: Random House, 1970.

Richards, John, *But Deliver Us from Evil: An Introduction to the Demonic in Pastoral Care.* New York: The Seabury Press, 1974.

Rogers, Carl R., *Client-Centered Therapy.* Boston: Houghton Mifflin Co., 1951.

————, *Freedom To Learn.* Columbus, Ohio: Charles E. Merrill Publishing Company, 1969.

Russell, Jeffrey B., *Witchcraft in the Middle Ages.* Ithaca, New York: Cornell University Press, 1972.

St. Clair, David, *Psychic Healers.* Garden City, New York: Doubleday & Company, Inc., 1974.

————, *Drum and Candle.* Garden City, New York: Doubleday & Company, 1971.

Sanford, John A., *Dreams: God's Forgotten Language.* Philadelphia: J. B. Lippincott Company, 1968.

————, *The Kingdom Within: A Study of the Inner Meaning of Jesus' Sayings.* Philadelphia: J. B. Lippincott Company, 1970.

Sargant, William, *Battle for the Mind.* Baltimore: Penguin Books, 1961.

Sartre, Jean-Paul, *Nausea.* New York: New Directions Publishing Corp., 1959.

————, *No Exit, and the Flies.* New York: Alfred A. Knopf, Inc., 1947.

A Select Library of the Nicene and Post-Nicene Fathers of the Christian Church. 1st and 2nd Series. Grand Rapids, Michigan: Wm. B. Eerdmans Publishing Co., various dates.

Sheehy, Gail, *Passages.* New York: E. P. Dutton & Co., Inc., 1976.

Skinner, B. F., *Beyond Freedom and Dignity.* New York: Alfred A. Knopf, Inc., 1971.

————, *Walden Two.* New York: The Macmillan Company, 1960.

Smith, Adam, *Powers of Mind.* New York: Random House, 1976.

Suenens, Léon Joseph, Cardinal, and Francis Martin, *A New Pentecost?* New York: The Seabury Press, 1975.

Sykes, Gerald, *The Hidden Remnant.* New York: Harper and Brothers, 1962.

Teilhard de Chardin, Pierre, *The Phenomenon of Man.* Harper & Brothers, 1959.

Thayer, Joseph Henry, *Greek-English Lexicon of the New Testament.* New York: American Book Company, 1889.

Theological and Pastoral Orientations of the Catholic Charismatic Renewal.

Malines, Belgium, 1974. Also Notre Dame, Indiana: Ave Maria Press, 1974.

Thomsen, Robert, *Bill W.* New York: Harper & Row, 1975.

Tolkien, J. R. R., *The Hobbit.* Boston: Houghton Mifflin Co., 1938.

——, *The Lord of the Rings* (Part I, *The Fellowship of the Ring*, Part II, *The Two Towers*, Part III, *The Return of the King*). Boston: Houghton Mifflin Co., 1954-55.

Von Franz, Marie-Louise, and Hillman, James, *Lectures on Jung's Typology.* New York: Spring Publications, 1970.

Watts, Alan (W.), *The Spirit of Zen.* New York: Grove Press, 1958.

——, *Tao: The Watercourse Way.* New York: Pantheon Books, 1975.

——, *The Two Hands of God: The Myths of Polarity.* New York: George Braziller, 1963.

Weil, Andrew, *The Natural Mind: A New Way of Looking at Drugs and the Higher Consciousness.* Boston: Houghton Mifflin Co., 1972.

Wheelwright, Joseph B., Ed., *The Reality of the Psyche.* New York: G. P. Putnam's Sons, 1968.

White, Victor, O.P., *God and the Unconscious.* Cleveland: The World Publishing Company, 1961.

Wickes, Frances F., *The Inner World of Childhood.* Rev. ed. New York: Appleton Century, 1966.

Wilkerson, David, and others, *The Cross and the Switchblade.* New York: Bernard Geis Associates, 1963.

Williams, Charles (W.), *Witchcraft.* New York: New American Library, 1959.

——, *Works (All Hallow's Eve, Descent into Hell, Many Dimensions, The Place of the Lion, Shadows of Ecstasy, War in Heaven).* Grand Rapids, Michigan: Wm. B. Eerdmans Publishing Co., 1965. (Also *Greater Trumps*, 1976).

Williams, Charles W., and Lewis, C. S., *Taliessin Through Logres, Region of the Summer Stars, the Arthurian Torso.* Grand Rapids, Michigan: Wm. B. Eerdmans Publishing Co., 1974.

Zimmer, Heinrich, *The King and the Corpse: Tales of the Soul's Conquest of Evil.* 2nd ed. Edited by Joseph Campbell. New York: Pantheon Books, 1956.